CONTINUING *the* RIDE

CRISSI
MCDONALD

FOREWORD BY MARK RASHID

CONTINUING
the RIDE

*Rebuilding Confidence
from the Ground Up*

Lilith House Press
Estes Park, Colorado

ISBN 978-1-7328258-3-3 (Softcover)
ISBN 978-1-7328258-4-0 (E-book)
Library of Congress Control Number: 2019915407

Neither the publisher nor the author is engaged in rendering professional
medical or therapeutic advice. The ideas and suggestions contained in
this book are not intended as a substitute for consulting with appropriate
and trained professionals. All matters regarding your health require
medical supervision. Neither the publisher nor the author shall be liable or
responsible for any loss or damage allegedly arising from any information or
suggestion in this book.

Cover and interior design: Jane Dixon-Smith/jdsmith-design.com
Editor: Susan Tasaki
Cover and author photograph: Lindsey Tedder

Printed and bound in the United States of America

For Mark, who has my heart.

And to all the horses and their people
who let me into their theirs.

The most difficult thing is the decision to act. The rest is merely tenacity. The fears are paper tigers. You can act to change and control your life; and the procedure, the process, is its own reward.

—Amelia Earhart

CONTENTS

Foreword   1

Introduction   5

One: New Horse, New Lessons   7

Two: Becoming a Detective   15

Three: The Unscheduled Dismount Club   19

Four: Finding the Herd   23

Five: Under the Rug   29

Six: It's Not the Fall, It's the Landing   37

Seven: The Pink Rose Cane   43

Eight: The Conversation   53

Nine: An Unruly Tomato Plant   59

Ten: Breath as a Bridge   65

Eleven: Ally Finds Us   69

Twelve: Homecoming   75

Thirteen: A Curious Mind   81

Fourteen: Hearing the Body   85

Fifteen: Fear Is Temporary   93

Sixteen: The Power of Movement   97

Seventeen: Pick a Direction   103

Eighteen: Continuing the Ride   111

Nineteen: Helmets   115

Twenty: Setbacks as Comebacks   121

Twenty-One: Changing Fear to Curiosity   125

Twenty-Two: Little Positives   131

Afterword: Full Circle   137

Thanks   141

Resources   143

FOREWORD

A couple of years ago, Crissi mentioned, almost in passing, that she was thinking about writing a book. She said she wanted it to be about how to emotionally recover from a serious horse accident. I thought, who better to write that book. After all, not only had Crissi experienced such an accident, but she had also spent years finding practical and effective ways to recover, both physically and mentally, from a fall that was serious enough to land her in the hospital.

Crissi began work on the book a short time later, and you are now holding in your hands the finished product, *Continuing the Ride*.

I remember thinking, after reading her almost-finished manuscript one night, that a lot of people are going to like and be helped by this book. Not only is it very well written, one of Crissi's trademarks, but it's also funny, thought-provoking and empowering. It's an amazing reference for folks looking to regain their confidence after an unfortunate horse mishap.

While this book is, indeed, all of those things, I believe it is actually much more, something deeper, something more like a love story. Let me explain.

Crissi and I met almost twenty years ago at a clinic I was doing in Arizona. She had brought her horse, Jack, a gray Missouri Fox Trotter that she rode bareback for her sessions. Jack was, how shall we say . . . a bit energetic. Still, one of the things I remember most about Crissi from that clinic was how much she smiled. If Jack was throwing himself around, she was smiling, if

1

he wouldn't stop, she smiled. If he would stop, she smiled. If she wanted to walk but he would gait, she smiled. If she wanted to gait and he would canter . . . well, you get the picture. On top of all that, not only did she smile whenever she was riding, but at least for me, that smile was contagious.

Throughout the weekend, Crissi asked a lot of questions. "How do you. . .?" "Why do you. . .?" "How does the horse know. . .?" Every question was accompanied by that same smile, and I remember thinking "That woman not only loves horses, but she loves everything about horses!"

From then on, Crissi would often show up at two or three clinics per year, and during that time, we slowly struck up a friendship based around our mutual love for horses. I would often find myself marveling at how Crissi would light up any-time she would tell me a story about Jack, the horse she had planned on buying and selling but ended up keeping for nearly twenty years, or her horse Zephyr, or any number of other horses she knew or had known.

Fast-forward a few years . . . Crissi and I found that our mutual love for horses had actually turned into a mutual love for each other, and eventually, we married. We have been through a lot together since that very first clinic all those years ago, but through it all, Crissi's smile, and her life-long love of horses, has never faltered.

That love was never more evident than in her actions follow-ing the accident that, quite frankly, would probably have been enough to stop a lot of people in their tracks. But not Crissi. With her, it became very clear very early on that her love for horses was going to outweigh the worry that was a by-product of her fall.

I watched in wonder as, only weeks after her fall and still walking with a cane, she insisted on getting on one of our old trustworthy geldings—bareback, because sitting in a saddle was still too painful. I watched as day after day and night after night, she sat at her computer researching brain science, how trauma affects the brain, how that translates to the body and most importantly, what to do about it. I watched as she tried acupuncture, chiropractic, physical therapy, and any number of other modalities of healing designed to help her regain both physical and spiritual balance, all just so she could get back to her one and only lifelong love: horses.

There is power in a love like that.

As time goes on, this book will undoubtedly come to mean many different things to many different people. Of that, I have no doubt. But to me, this book will always be just one thing . . .

A Love Story. One that began many years ago with a little girl on a borrowed pony, and continuing on to this day with Crissi, still smiling, living a life filled with horses.

Mark Rashid
Estes Park, Colorado

INTRODUCTION

When I was still in diapers, I met a Shetland pony. From the look on my face in the picture, it was love at first sight. Like my smile, I may have inherited my love of horses from my mom. She remembers a boy she liked and galloping with him across the desert on one of his family's ranch horses. The freedom of that gallop and the horse she rode has outlasted the memory of the boy.

As I grew up, I sought the company of horses. I rode my bike and pretended it was a horse. I found horses not far from where I lived and snuck grass to them through the fence. It was liberating to discover that they didn't care about the things I saw reflected in my peers' eyes; they didn't judge or assess or withhold their regard because my clothes weren't trendy or I wore glasses or had a last name they could make a joke about. They responded to silence. They sought out kindness. They smelled good. I was, and still am, hooked.

The descriptor "horse-crazy" is endearing when applied to a pre-teen girl. When said about an adult, it can mean something else entirely. As in, no one understands, and thinks you must be more than a little crazy when you keep going back to these big, lightning-fast animals after enduring stepped-on toes; broken bones; hitting the ground; and, in some cases (like mine), a brain bleed. Or worse.

What I'd like to offer you with this book is essentially a blueprint—a way to begin to get off the ground and untangle what has happened as a result of an accident with a horse so you can help yourself feel better. What I share are guidelines of sorts, things I've found interesting and that were helpful in my own steps back to confidence. Take or leave anything, or use these ideas to forge a different path for yourself.

Woven into the story is what I've learned about trauma, brain function, and how to make the best of what you've got. One of my more important lessons was that feelings of intense anxiety and fear aren't permanent. They don't have to interfere with enjoying horses, and they especially don't have to stop you from having horses in your life, unless you choose not to.

From my personal experience and the experiences of the people I've had the honor of instructing who also are frustrated by fear, I cannot say that what you will find here will enable you to ride "fear-free." Maybe there is such a thing, but that has not been my experience. Riding with less fear, however? That's well within the reach of us all.

Much of my life, I've let fear dictate what I do, or avoid doing. But I recently turned fifty and have decided that as I move into this next phase, I'd like to take the bullhorn away from my fear's blabbermouth. I'm okay with maintaining a healthy sense of caution around horses, but fear can speak with its inside voice now.

I'm not a therapist and haven't any plans to be one. What I am is stubborn and curious. These traits have generally served me well, never more so than when I had to face the long road back to feeling joyful and at ease with horses once again.

I hope that within these pages, you'll find something that helps you as you rebuild and rediscover your own confidence.

ONE

NEW HORSE, NEW LESSONS

February 4, 2014

I'm dreaming of silver-gray fog and horses running through it. Their tails are tendrilled clouds, their heads are high and nostrils wide. I hear the echo of a whinny. I feel their hooves drumming the earth through the length of my body.

I thought it was morning, and I was waking from a dream of horses.

It was mid-afternoon, and I was regaining consciousness after my mare flipped over backward, crushing my right leg beneath the saddle and her panicked hooves.

Five Years Earlier

Standing in the round pen was a delicate bay Arabian mare. She had a bushy black mane and eyes that were squinty and hard. She wasn't interested in the person at the other end of the lead rope and this got me wondering what was troubling her.

She was seven years old, and from what we could gather, was mainly ridden at a canter or gallop around a local track. Owned by some older folks who needed to disperse their herd of Arabians, this little mare needed a new home.

Our friend Carla had borrowed her to bring to a clinic Mark

and I were teaching. Carla didn't plan on getting on a horse, or going fast when she did get on, so she wisely decided to practice groundwork with the mare. After four days of watching our friend work on skills that were new to both of them, we came to admire the horse's temperament—she didn't get upset even when she was unsure. Mark and I thought that with time and education, she might turn out to be a pretty good clinic horse. We decided we could take her; after the paperwork was done and she was standing in the paddock with our other two horses, I named her Breagha (Bree), Gaelic for "lovely."

A clinic horse's job isn't as easy as it appears. If you attend one of our clinics, you would see quiet horses going through their day, alternately standing tied or being ridden by the instructor. There's usually not a lot of dust being raised; our horses rarely move faster than a steady jog. There's a lot of stopping and standing still. You would see that on rainy days, they're covered with waterproof sheets and stand around eating. They get hay at lunch and extra supplements after their workday is finished.

What you don't see are the thousands of trailer miles these horses have spent inside an aluminum and steel box, blindly bumping along, leaning into unseen turns, and sometimes, when traffic isn't cooperative, covering the miles an inch at a time. You don't feel the hot days that raise a sweat despite a breeze through the open trailer windows or hear the gunshot staccato beat of a hailstorm or the howling of the wind as we outrace tornado clouds across the Nebraska prairie.

When we reach our destination, our horses are usually unloaded in the dark. We prefer they have a large paddock or field to overnight in, but will put them in a stall if the weather is cranky. Most overnight stops are new, so they don't know the sights, the sounds, or the smells. We'll leave in the morning before they've had a chance to familiarize themselves with anything more than the current temperature and the shape of the space they're in.

For clinic horses, a few skills are mandatory. They need to get into and out of a trailer without worry at any time of the day or night, in any location, rain or shine. They need to be able to stand still with a rider on their back. They need to feel okay about standing tied for hours.

Our clinic horses have to be comfortable with other horses around them, possibly bumping into them, as well as stay calm when another horse needs to move a lot or whinny to relieve stress.

This is a big ask for any animal, particularly one that has lived in herds for millions of years, and not every horse can do it. If we find that a horse doesn't have the physical strength or the emotional flexibility to do this job, we find a good home for them.

When Mark and I decided to give Bree a home, we saw a little bay mare with a whole lot of clinic-horse potential. As I got Bree out that first day, I didn't know which horse she would be: the calm and quiet one who could live on the road most of the year, or the horse who needed more stability and familiar surroundings. I was excited to get to know her and find out.

My excitement arose because I would be experiencing a lot of firsts, probably right along with Bree. Bree was the first clinic horse I would be bringing along myself. Although I'd started colts and ridden a lot of horses, I'd never had a chance to show them how to do this particular job. It was also the first time I would be teaching people at the same time as I was helping my horse. I'd worked with other owners and horses, helping them both feel better, but never while riding one of my own horses. Although I'd spent a lot of time with Arabians while I was in high school, Bree was the first Arabian I would get to know and live with.

So, here she was, Bree the lovely bay mare, the unwitting recipient of my emotions, ambitions, and dreams. It's almost comical, looking back, to realize that as I thought I was "helping" Bree, what was truly going on was that she was showing me my own vanities and assumptions. To be fair, she also taught me where my skills were—and where they weren't.

When we get a new horse, we don't know each other; generally, all we have is the previous owner's side of the story. So, we spend time showing them what they need to know to do their job. This is not only the horse's chance to get to know us, it's also our time to get to know the horse.

When we went out on the first morning of the clinic to get our horses ready for their workday, I started gathering information about Bree. How did she feel about two humans, halters jingling at their sides, coming into her pen? Answer: not comfortable. She swung her head away and walked in the opposite direction. As Mark caught his horse and stood with him, I followed Bree, walking parallel to her line of travel. When she stopped, I did, too. I waited for a breath before approaching her again, the jingling halter blasting my intention, and she stood still, her black-tipped brown ears not quite pinned back.

We took the horses to the trailer, tied them, and began to groom them. Bree swung to the left and right, agitated and unable to stand still. I moved with her, and at one point when I couldn't move anymore, I brought my arm up to her ribcage to block her swing. This startled her enough that she swung the opposite way, right into Mark's horse, who, with a foot stomp, pinned ears, and a swing back into her, made it clear he wouldn't be banged into.

Bree stood still.

I love horse communication. Mark's horse, an expert in how to get through a workday, saved me a lot of time and being bumped into by making that boundary clear.

After Bree was groomed, I made sure my saddle fit her, then hung my bridle on the wide horn and untied her so we could walk to the arena. As Mark started teaching and I was waiting for my student at the opposite side of the arena, I decided to see how Bree felt about my foot in the stirrup.

Standing on her left side, I raised my left foot into the stirrup and looked at her. She ever-so-slightly rocked back on her hind-quarters, not-so-slightly pinned her ears, and then tried to leave the ground like a rocket.

I decided I didn't need to ride that day.

Days turned into weeks as we taught clinics. Every morning, I brought Bree out, groomed her, saddled her up, hung the bridle on the horn of my saddle, and led her out to the arena we would be in for the day.

Every day, I put my foot in the stirrup and prepared to mount. I would wait until her dancing stopped, hopping one-legged beside her as I kept my lead rope short. I was glad I had taken up yoga.

Each day, she showed less anxiety and less need to run. Every day, there was an improvement. I thought, "Well, she's an Arab and they're noted for being extra-intelligent." I thought, "Well, the supplements she's getting are helping her." I thought, "Horses are amazing and brilliant."

Now, all of these are true. And, every thought I had about why she was settling so quickly after years of being inadvertently taught to run when the rider's foot hit the stirrup was only part of the picture.

During those weeks, circumstances conspired to give her a

lot of time. Since I had other things to do, she and I could only work sporadically on this one skill. As a result, she was able to settle from a chronically stressed state into a more relaxed frame of mind, which allowed her learning to be more firmly cemented. Horses learn best when pressure is low and intermittent, and this meant that she could integrate the information and start to build confidence in our interactions.

That summer, we traveled from Colorado to New Hampshire. Bree was proving to be an eager and hardy clinic horse. She got in and out of a trailer without any trouble. She led well and was calm and confident and finished her hay both on the trailer and off. There was a light blooming in her eyes, and she was now calm about being caught, groomed, saddled, and bridled. We'd had a chiropractor check her out, and her feet and teeth were taken care of as well. I knew my saddle and pad were a good fit.

Three months had gone by since we started working together, and I was able to not only get on her, but her dancing around while I was on her back was almost non-existent. Now, it was a matter of helping her feel better about standing still.

I'd discovered that Bree also didn't understand how to turn right or left, or how to stop. So as I taught students and their horses, I was also teaching Bree. We'd walk with them on the inside of a circle as we talked about what we were working on.

On a hot New Hampshire summer day, I asked Bree to stop, and then carried on teaching. She let out a long sigh, cocked a hind leg, put her head and neck down low, closed her eyes, and stayed that way. I was so mesmerized by this change in her that I got off and stood while I taught the rest of the lesson.

After that day, she did everything in a more relaxed state of mind. It was as though she hadn't known it was possible to go slowly once a rider was on her back, but when she discovered it, she liked it. She liked standing still and being quiet so much that people would ask me if she was a purebred Arabian, since what most people see of Arabs is a human-manufactured tendency to be fiery and excitable. Bree went through the days slowly and thoughtfully.

I've always figured that a horse is a horse, and horses are, by nature and evolution, quiet animals. If they weren't, there would be a lot fewer of them hoofing it across the earth and many more in the bellies of big predators. The argument about a horse being a certain way because of its breed doesn't hold much weight as far as I'm concerned.

What is essential, both with Bree then and with any horse I come across now, is that they feel safe and are comfortable in their minds and bodies. Horses are horses first and a breed or gender second. The moment we start treating horses as their breed or their gender, we miss a valuable opportunity to get to know them better. Labeling anything and adding assumptions don't usually lead to innovation and deep insight. By doing the best we can to see what is in front of us as it is, we can generally find a way to get along.

By listening to our horses, we gain an amazing education. It was a lengthy process for me to realize the importance of this skill, and how to apply it. It began in the late 1990s when I had just started training horses, with a colt and his owner, John.

TWO

BECOMING A DETECTIVE

June 1997

When I began working with Arrow, he was a fresh-off-the-range Quarter Horse colt. His owner, John, while experienced, was old enough to want to avoid hitting the ground. After talking about the goals he had for himself and his horse, we settled on a schedule: I'd come out twice a week and he would do ground-work with Arrow in between.

By that time, I'd started a handful of colts and was feeling confident that I could help Arrow too. Arrow spent a month learning about longeing and ropes, saddle pads and saddles. At the end of a month, he could carry a bridle and saddle at a walk, trot, and canter without any worry. Although suspicious at first, he settled down once he knew what was going on.

The next week, I climbed up on the rusty round pen fence and worked with him until he was quiet with me above him. After that, from the ground, I started putting my foot in the stirrup and my body over his back. He had a little more trouble here, and it took longer than I expected to help him quiet down.

By this time, John, usually a patient man and happy to be going slowly, asked when I thought I'd be getting on and doing some riding. He had trails he wanted to cover that fall and he thought Arrow would take to that kind of job.

The next session with Arrow was spent with the idea of me

getting on and riding. We had taken it slowly. Made sure he was feeling okay. He would work his way out of feeling squirrelly with a rider on his back, I thought.

I introduced this idea of getting on as I always did. As he always did, Arrow moved and tried to get out from under the weight. We stayed in a small circle, and I waited until he was still before releasing him and walking him around. Then we tried again.

This is where I made two mistakes: I let another person's agenda become more important than what the horse had to say, and I slipped into conqueror mode. You know the feeling: a puffy-chested, inflexible mental stance we take when We Shall Win. It's as old as people in caves. So I slung my leg over the saddle, sat down, and expected Arrow to comply.

Arrow didn't. True to his name, he went forward. Very quickly. Then he went up and down four times. I sat out the first three jumps. The fourth, in which he added a twist toward the fence, rocketed me face-first into the dirt in the middle of the pen.

As I got up, mentally assessing how my body felt and happy that the dirt disguised how red my face was, I knew I'd made a big mistake. I watched Arrow, who was now standing and facing me; he seemed as surprised as I was by the whole thing. I walked over to him and patted him on his neck. He breathed deeply and lowered his head. I led him around, and then removed his saddle and made sure nothing on it or the pad had hurt him.

There was nothing on the pad, and the western saddle fit well and was sound. The flocked underside showed nothing that could have poked him. I stood back and looked at Arrow and for the first time, saw that one of his shoulders was a little larger than the other at the top. I walked over to him and started running my fingers down his back where the saddle went, applying pressure. He sank out from underneath the pressure on both sides. His withers were also sore. My conqueror mindset shifted to detective mode.

I learned a lesson with Arrow that continues to serve me to this day. What I had once seen and felt as a failure had transformed into an education. This was the day I started paying more attention to the horse and letting my conqueror (in whose world there is only Win or Lose) sit at the back of the class.

John and I decided to schedule an equine massage therapist to work on Arrow. In the 1990s, this was a rare thing, and to a working cowboy, it must have sounded like I wanted to fly Arrow to the moon.

She came out three times that month to work on Arrow. After she thought he was doing better, he and I started the saddling and riding process from the beginning. It didn't take long before he was right where he was before he'd lived up to his name. After two weeks had gone by, I found myself with a foot in the stirrup, ready to get on.

I also felt the first tremblings of "don't do this." Fear was knocking on my door, quietly but there, for the first time in my young-trainer life. This time, however, I slowed down. I looked at Arrow, trying to see if he thought this was a good idea. I put my hands on him, as much to reassure myself as to comfort him. Then, when we were both feeling a bit more calm, I once again slid my leg over and sat down as gently as I could.

"You're both gonna turn blue if you don't take a breath soon," John laughed. I laughed, too, taking a breath and smiling. Arrow, with the innate genius all horses have, also took a breath, shook his head, and stood still.

This time, I had John come into the pen and lead Arrow around. After a few minutes, John let go of the reins and Arrow continued to follow him. I dismounted, and John and I stood chatting about whether to call it a day or not. I looked at Arrow, who was still bright-eyed and relaxed, and decided to get on one more time and see how he felt about walking on his own.

Turns out, walking on his own with me on his back wasn't that big a deal. Before the month was out, John was riding him all over his property. Within another month, they were in the mountains trail-riding. As far as I know, Arrow and John still are out having fun together.

That wasn't the first time I'd come off a horse, but it was the first time I'd realized that it could have been avoided if I hadn't ignored what Arrow had been trying to tell me. With quite a bit of embarrassment, I finally understood that I had been training horses like one of those people who continually interrupts a conversation. After not being able to get a word in or complete a thought, you either wait to see if this person will run out of air and pause for breath, or you find a polite way to leave.

Arrow didn't have the luxury of leaving. At that time in my life, I didn't have the skill to pause. The only choice he had left was to act on instinct—as all horses will if they are scared or hurt.

Since I'd assumed that what I had to say was more important than what Arrow had to say, he showed me in as clear a way as he could why this assumption was wrong.

I'd come off several times before I met Arrow and had always blamed the horse. Consequently, I didn't learn much from the experiences.

Except for the first time, when I was ten years old. Up to that point, I'd only ridden fantasy horses in my waking dreams.

THREE
THE UNSCHEDULED DISMOUNT CLUB

Horse dreams aren't easily knocked out of us. Their compelling call keeps many of us tethered to the sound of galloping hooves, to the hay sweetness of their breath, even when the thought arises that maybe this horse thing isn't working out so well.

When we have an accident with a horse, most of us will say that it happened too quickly to do anything about it. This is true. Loss of details, loss of memory, and loss of the exact moment of injury are the brain and body's way of protecting us. Even when remembering the first time I came off a Shetland pony named Moonlight, all I have left are images, not feelings about them. So, while this story is true, shock and time have erased much of it.

Owned by a friend of my mother's, Moonlight was dark and dappled gray, with a flaxen mane and tail and eyes the color of a dark, clear pond. She nuzzled, she nickered, and her coat was silky. She smelled of oats and summer grasses. As I sat on her round back, all my ten-year-old horse dreams came true. Then I gave a little kick with my short legs and asked her to move.

Tossing her dainty nose in the air, she took off, heading straight for a framed-in barn, with me gripping her mane for all I was worth. Too late, I saw a cross beam coming up fast, straight toward my face. A voice sounded in my head—my mom, saying, "Glasses are expensive." I did the only thing I could think of: I let go of Moonlight's mane and covered my face, protecting my glasses. I hit the crossbeam and slid off her back onto the ground, like Wile E. Coyote sliding down a cliff. Moonbeam galloped on.

I couldn't breathe, but my glasses weren't broken. When I could breathe, I cried. It was my first clue that even small horses can do big things.

My mother and her friend gathered me up, and after I caught my breath, they returned me to Moonlight's silky gray back and led me around the enclosure. In an astonishing leap of faith, they then had me ride her by myself. Looking back, I think Moonlight was done running for the day and ready for a meal.

This was my initiation into the Unscheduled Dismount Club. It's quite a large club. We don't have slogans, meeting places, or social media pages, but we number in the millions. We're joined by that moment when we unexpectedly parted company with our horse.

If we've been riding for any length of time, we know the rule: after a fall, get back on the horse. If an ambulance is involved, we have an out. Otherwise, up we go. While this rule is handed out by well-meaning horsemen and women, it's not always the most helpful solution. And because we're in shock, we will sometimes do things that aren't in our best interest. Like riding a horse before we've recovered.

When we bypass the process of working through injury-caused shock, when we believe we have to "suck it up," "be brave," or any of the other variations on those themes, the energy of the shock and trauma gets stored in our bodies and psyches. Over time, we may experience a cascade of sensations when we're near a horse: our breathing might get shallow, our hands might get cold, we might notice our heart racing like we just sprinted a mile. We may not be able to think clearly. We may feel like crying or look for excuses not to ride. From here, it's a short distance to feeling incompetent and ashamed, hopeless and frustrated with ourselves.

There's another way to look at it, however. A horse-related shock or injury—whether it takes place on the ground or while riding—is like getting a splinter in your finger. There's the initial shock of the pain. We give all our attention to removing the splinter, and once it's out, we shake our hand rapidly. The same thing happens if we hit one of our fingers with a hammer: the injury happens, there's pain, we focus our attention on the damage, and we disperse the energy of the shock.

This is, in perhaps a simplistic way, the same process our bodies and minds need to go through to complete the cycle and, most importantly, to let it go. The injury happens. There is the result of the injury. Our attention goes to what just happened. We then need to move to disperse and release it. After an accident on a horse, we will give our attention to the first two of these needs and bypass the third. Sometimes, it's because we can't or shouldn't move, but by the time we can do something about it, we have convinced ourselves that we are okay, all is well, and we move on.

Immediately going back to the horse, or riding, isn't necessarily a bad or wrong choice. But I believe we could benefit from slowing that process down a bit. As instructors, we could give our students the time they need to recover their wits and discharge the shock. If we're the one who's just had an accident, we could give ourselves permission to ride again immediately, or not. We need to allow our body to run through its process so that if we do get back on that horse, we are in a thinking frame of mind rather than just going through the motions. Because every person and every accident is different, this process can take anywhere from five minutes to five months or longer.

When moving through an injury is interrupted by our not

being able to move, much like a splinter that's never taken out, the body and mind create walls around the injury. It doesn't, however, stop the pain. This pain gets rerouted and has been proven to show up as mental fog, chronic low-level anxiety, depression, and lack of energy for life, among other things.

I don't know about you, but these are the kind of houseguests I would prefer had a limited stay.

Thankfully, when it comes to horses, it's not all trauma and accidents and trips to the hospital. It's also wonderment and awe that seal memories inside you for the rest of your life.

FOUR

FINDING THE HERD

June 1990

Before I decided to train horses, in my early twenties I was hired by a Girl Scout camp in New Mexico to be their riding director. This included not only watching after the welfare of more than thirty horses for the summer, but also overseeing a team of three other wranglers as well as giving riding lessons and setting up fun activities for sixteen pre-teen and teenage campers every hour.

Our herd was leased from a ranch in Colorado. One of their wranglers, Deena, came with them to join our team and help us get to know the horses.

At the end of their time at camp, we took the girls on a trail ride and overnight pack trip as a way to celebrate everything they had learned.

The trail ride day started out like any other. My team of wranglers and I groomed and saddled up twenty horses, including our own. We checked that the saddles and blankets were on the right horses, made sure the tack was clean and the cinches were tight before matching each girl to her horse and helping her climb on.

My horse that summer was a mare named Bess. The previous year's riding director had changed it from Witch because, like me, she didn't want to call a horse such a demeaning name.

Bess was a dun mare with a dark brown line down her back, a honey-blond coat, and a square head. She carried her ears to the side and she demanded fair treatment from her rider. Her black mane was shot through with light brown streaks and her hooves were every horse person's dream: large, black, and seemingly made to scale mountains. She moved with purpose. I liked her right away.

She could be counted on to get me next to a horse and rider who couldn't move or to demonstrate how to run a barrel pattern. She charged through the river we went across on our trail rides, and by sheer presence alone, kept the other horses in line.

She also helped me to become a better rider. She was a literalist: I couldn't give any signal I didn't mean. An ounce more leg than I intended? We went faster. Holding the reins a little too long in the stop? We went backward. Not paying attention to my balance? She'd pin her ears and list in the opposite direction, reminding me to sit in the middle and stay out of her way.

At the head of the line, with my wranglers scattered throughout the group of chattering girls, we made our way down a trail I'd taken only once before. Thankfully, Deena had also been on this ride the previous year, and she guided us whenever we came to a turn.

Morning turned into early afternoon, and the shadows of the trees didn't offer much shade as we rode through them. I could hear not only the rumblings of hungry girl stomachs but of my own, too. After we reached our campsite, we got everyone dismounted and sent the girls with their camp counselor to start on lunch.

We tied the horses, pulled saddles, brushed sweat off wet horse backs, and turned the herd into a large pole corral. As each found a dusty soft spot to roll in, I took a moment to admire the sheen and variety of their coats. There were bay horses and chestnut horses, a black horse, a paint horse, and a gray roan pony called Shorty whom I not-so-secretly wanted to take home with me. Tall and rangy, short and round, horses with flowing manes and tails and an Appaloosa with a switch for a tail and a mane that barely sprouted from his thin neck. After they had rolled, shown their teeth and laid back their ears at one another, they all had a drink and then found the hay we had thrown into piles for them.

The afternoon was spent eating lunch, setting up camp, talking about how to keep bears away from the food, rules and guidelines and fire safety. Every so often, I would go check on the horses, as much from a need to bask in their beauty as to make sure they had enough water or that the gate was latched.

When the sun's rays were slanting over our small field and the girlish chatter had quieted down, Deena suggested we turn the horses out to graze. Skeptical, I asked if they all wouldn't just head back to the barn without us. Deena assured me that they did this all the time at the horses' home ranch, and that as long as we hobbled the lead horses, the rest would stay close by. With this in mind, I agreed with Deena's suggestion. We brought the herd's lead horses—including Bess—out of the corral, hobbled them, took off their halters, and watched as they lowered their heads to eat. Then we opened the gate. After wary glances and some snorting sideways head tilts, the rest of the herd streamed through the gap.

Some stopped to graze, some stopped to sniff their companions who were hobbled, and some continued to walk, looking in the direction where camp must have been. Shorty and two other horses kept walking. Two more lifted their heads and, after a moment of flicking their ears back and forth, followed them.

Before we could say whoa, all the loose horses started moving toward those who were now trotting back the way we had come that morning. Even a couple of the hobbled horses were hopping like rabbits, trying to catch up.

With Bess's halter in hand, I walked up to her as quietly as I could and put it on her. She was concerned but didn't strain against being caught. She stood still as another wrangler caught the horse that was grazing near Bess. Out of breath and red-faced, Deena came up to me and said she'd boost me up on Bess's back so I could go after the herd, which was now galloping toward home. The only sign that they had been there was the dust settling onto the road in sun-streaked lines and the row of old western saddles propped against the corral.

We unhobbled Bess and as she started to dance around, Deena pitched me up onto her back. I had the lead rope in my left hand and Bess's black mane clutched in my right.

For the first time in my life, I realized I was entirely at the mercy of a horse.

No saddle. No bridle. No way to control movement or speed or direction. What little Bess and I knew of each other was about to be tested.

She quickly turned to her right and picked up a lope from a standstill. She whinnied once, pricked her ears forward, and shifted into a long gallop. She found a road I didn't know existed and followed it, her gallop slowing as she encountered a fresh pile of manure. After lowering her head to sniff it, she picked up her gallop again.

Once I got over my initial shock at how fast we were going, I found that riding a gallop bareback was actually easy. As I relaxed and went with her, my death grip on her mane loosened and I gathered up the tail end of the lead rope. My only job now was to stay balanced and keep the rope from interfering with her.

A fork in the road was coming up. I knew better than to use my lead rope to try and influence her direction. I didn't know where I was and was riding bareback on a horse who had more answers than I did.

Bess picked up her head, whinnied, and listened, never slowing down to less than a lope. She then veered right and again shifted into a gallop. I noticed that her breathing was labored and her stride not quite as long. But she felt relaxed under me and the rhythm of the gait allowed me to settle in and make a note of where we were.

I saw another pile of manure ahead of us. This time, Bess

stopped and smelled it for several seconds before loping off and following the road around a bend to the left.

Two minutes later, I saw the first signs of a cluster of horses. They were milling around in a circle like fish in a net. There were also people around them, and I recognized my boss standing away from the group and scratching her head. I reflected on how much I'd enjoyed my gallop with Bess, and that it might have been the last ride for me that summer.

My knees were shaking as I dismounted, then gathered the lead rope and went to talk to my boss and figure out our next steps. Two of the wranglers rode up, each carrying an armload of halters. We caught all the horses, and the four of us spent the evening leading them back to the campsite and back into the corral. The rest of the trip was uneventful.

Turns out I wasn't fired, but Deena was under strict orders not to graze the horses in an open field. For my part, I'll never forget how it felt to surrender and fly with Bess as she found her way back to the herd. I'll always remember how it felt to almost be a horse.

UNDER THE RUG

We often have people show up at a clinic who are afraid of their horse, afraid to ride, or both. Although they're desperate to ride, they can't force themselves anymore. Oftentimes, they find other things to do with their horses: going on hikes, doing groundwork, or simply being with them, all of which are great options.

When we start asking questions, we usually hear about not only a big accident, but everything else that happened before. Broken wrists, ribs, legs, and backs, severe concussions, almost bleeding out, being paralyzed. Yet these courageous people continue to push through, to find a way to be around horses in spite of it feeling like a life-or-death choice.

One person who had made this choice was Sally, a retired military pilot. I met her while I was teaching at a clinic in Utah.

"So, what would you like to work on today?" I asked.

"Well," she said, looking at her bay gelding, "I think Shiloh is a nice horse, but I'm not sure he's a good match for me. I haven't really ridden in a while, and I'd like your opinion about whether I should keep or sell him."

Looking at the gelding, bridled, saddled, and napping in the sun, I asked, "How long have you been around horses, and what have you done?"

Sally became animated, gesturing and talking rapidly as she told me that while growing up, she had ridden English, and then discovered three-day eventing. She loved Thoroughbreds and Thoroughbred crosses. But although they were big and bold, not all of them were as athletic as she had assumed, and sometimes, there were accidents. Then Sally fulfilled her dream of becoming a pilot, and horses took second place. She'd ridden off and on through adulthood, and since retiring had returned to horses, though mostly trail riding with friends because jumping didn't feel as exciting anymore.

"I guess after going Mach 1, jumping kind of lost its excitement," she laughed. "But I sure don't miss the injuries!"

"How many accidents have you had?" I asked.

She smiled, her brown eyes clouding over. "I don't have an exact number."

I noticed that she was holding her breath.

"Would you say more than ten? More than twenty?"

She became quiet as she thought about this number. Even though the day was warm, she wrapped her arms around her torso.

"Probably more than ten, but less than twenty?" Sally wasn't smiling now, and she looked at her horse. "I don't get it. Six months ago, I was trail riding on Shiloh and he tripped over a rock. I didn't come off, but I don't remember the rest of the ride."

Curious, I asked, "Do you remember anything else happening before or after that?"

"It's stupid, really," she shook her head. "He stepped on my foot because something scared him. My foot wasn't broken, but man, did it bruise. I couldn't wear my boots for a week."

"How long is it since you've ridden?" I asked.

"Two months. But I get him out almost every day and groom him. I just . . . don't feel like riding. Maybe a different horse would help."

I've learned that trauma is not just one thing; it can be everything that happened before. Your body and brain work together to store all sorts of information. What happened doesn't go away, even after we physically heal. If we don't move all the way through it and instead sweep it under our internal rugs, what we feel and how we respond to our horses and our lives will begin to accumulate.

We become unintentional trauma hoarders. How it looks varies from person to person, but some of the signs that we've been busy sweeping include shallow breathing, low-level (but quickly switched to high-level) anxiety, avoidance of activities or nervousness while doing them, cold hands or feet, or procrastination about an activity involving horses or anything that feels threatening.

I can say this with certainty because even before my horse flipped over backward that day in 2014, I was noticing the not-so-subtle signs that all was not well. I was hesitant to work with certain horses. I had trouble sleeping. Thoughts would take root in my brain and I couldn't stop them from lapping around and around and around. Even as I was teaching people about the power of long, deep breaths, I felt chronically nervous. It didn't escape me that I needed to follow my own advice.

Finally, weary of my own pattern, I kicked my stubbornness and curiosity into high gear. I binged on research about what happens when we experience trauma as children. I read about human brain anatomy. About the latest findings on diet, exercise, and supplementation to calm chronic anxiety. This information was beyond useful; I found answers to why I felt the way I did and did things that seemed a little off-kilter. It was the first time in my life that I had researched and devoted time to finding out how I ticked—how we all tick.

The day I hit the ground in 2014 was one of the most significant wake-up calls of my life. I didn't know it then, but it was going to be my chance to stop sweeping and stop ignoring a rug that by now was not really covering all the junk beneath it. In fact, this internal rug had so much stuffed under it that it was blocking my way to being able to get out the door and be with horses.

I find it the height of irony that we are our own internal housekeepers, yet we wonder, "Who put that sofa over there? Where did that lamp come from? Who thought it was a good idea to leave the dirt under this rug?"

I believe that an unexamined sense of failure is where the rule "Thou Shalt Get Back on Thy Horse" mainly comes from. We can't stand it; we won't be able to sleep or eat another tasty morsel of anything until we prove we haven't failed. If coming off a horse or getting hurt by one is a failure, then getting back up or getting back on is the win. It's the oldest trick in our subterranean brain's book: given a choice between winning and losing, we all want to be winners. So we stuff things in our internal room or under our interior mental rug and we pretend it isn't there.

When I first started riding, coming off a horse brought up immediate shame, especially when I was a teenager and humiliation is a constant threat to be avoided. The "You're not good enough to do this," sneaky mean tape played over and over. And over. I strived to prove it wrong because if I was thinking it, surely others were, too. At this point, what my horse thought of the whole business may as well have been another universe.

This began changing once I started focusing on who the horse was. Who is this large animal? What's important to him? Why do horses do what they do?

Knowledge and education are powerful forces against ignorance. They are also great at dispelling assumptions and false beliefs. I found this out because, in the process of learning more about horses, I also discovered just how many false beliefs I was carrying from my time learning from various trainers—how many beliefs I had taken from others and added to the pile under my own mental rug.

Here are a few of those false beliefs, and I bet some of them sound familiar: "Show the horse who's boss." "Make him do it; don't let him get away with that." "Make that horse collect." "You gotta do a thousand repetitions before a horse learns what you want."

From what I've learned—and continue to learn—none of those statements have any basis in truth or fact. Horses are smart. They don't need bosses, they need leaders. Making a horse do something is a far harsher process than asking or helping, and a thousand repetitions of any skill mindlessly repeated can only cause a horse to be dull.

So, not only does the accumulation of trauma happen and get in the way of us enjoying our horse, rigid beliefs do as well.

It's my opinion that knowledge, understanding, and empathy create more room for the horses in our lives. Rigid beliefs and reliance on others' opinions often leave such a narrow space for the horse to occupy that we end up looking at them as humans in horse suits rather than horses.

Most of the time, you can tell how people handle their horses by the way horses are themselves. Those who are treated as horses are usually relaxed or settle quickly even when they're nervous. Their eyes are bright and they're at ease in the presence of people. They're generally pretty easy to catch and handle.

If they aren't any of these things, once you show them what is expected of them, the process goes relatively smoothly and they cooperate. Here's what I've noticed: horses are hardwired to get along. They don't have the ability to deceive themselves or others like we do.

If we've swept away things we'd rather not look at or deal with, that's on us.

As for Sally and Shiloh, I thought we could look at a couple of simple solutions before making any big decisions about selling her horse.

After we chatted about how our bodies react to injury or fright, I shared a simple way to feel better. I asked her to take a brisk walk leading Shiloh around the arena.

"This is something I learned from therapists and from my studies, and do when I feel nervous. Taking a brisk walk does a couple of things. It gets your body moving instead of freezing in fear, and it causes you to breathe more deeply."

Sally looked skeptical but smiled before striding off through the deep sand of the arena. After one lap, she smiled again and asked if it was okay to stop now.

"Well," I answered, "how's your breathing? And is the nervousness you're feeling any better?"

She thought for a moment before shaking her head and asked if I would hold Shiloh while she walked.

"It's the weirdest thing," she said. "I really feel like running."

"Then run. When you don't feel like it anymore, go back to walking."

Sally started off at a jog, but then quickly accelerated into a run for two laps, before stopping in front of me, leaning over with her hands on her knees and gasping for breath.

"I think I can stop now," she panted.

"Good!" I was pleased that she was visibly more relaxed.

As she worked on breathing deeply, I explained that in the future, it would be a good idea to either walk or run before she went out to see Shiloh. We also talked about her looking into finding a therapist who could take her into what she was going through with more skilled guidance than a horse trainer could provide.

"Breathing, coupled with movement, will go a lot further in helping you feel better than being stationary and feeling so much fear," I said. "And you don't have to ride—today or any other day—so give some thought to removing that pressure from yourself. Breathe and move, and at the very least, you'll feel much better. So will Shiloh—although," I said, as I looked at him napping in the sun, "I have a feeling that he's a pretty okay guy."

She grinned, and for the first time during our session, I saw her face relax and her eyes soften.

"Yes, that's why I like him so much. I think he's really going to help me work through this. I was just feeling so crummy that I thought I needed to sell him. But maybe not."

I've often wondered what kind of effect it has on horses when we enter their space and we aren't breathing deeply. I have seen countless times how even quiet horses will startle easily and move with tension if the person around or on them is essentially holding their breath. Conversely, I have also seen how reclaiming our innately nourishing deep breath can help a horse calm down, just as in the case of Sally and Shiloh.

Here's an observation: if you are standing in the middle of a group of horses and they are startled by something, the only things you will hear are environmental sounds; maybe some birdsong or some far-off traffic noise. Maybe the wind.

No chewing on hay, no wuff of soft breath.

Horses on alert stop breathing. Their eyes and ears are forward and their nostrils dilated. They stop moving. They listen, and look, and decode their surroundings to decide whether to stay put or run.

When that decision is made, they will either move as far away as possible from the threat or they will breathe again, maybe a big snort of air before they lower their heads and continue to eat.

Breathing is free. You can do it anytime, anywhere, and almost no one will notice. There's nothing to sign up for, no equipment to buy, and it won't make you more susceptible to spam, computer viruses, or phishing scams. The benefits are far-reaching, and no matter how many times you forget it to do it, you can always reconnect and breathe more deeply, right now. Your body, and your horse, will thank you.

SIX

IT'S NOT THE FALL,
IT'S THE LANDING

July 2011

Mark and I were in New Hampshire again. We had three horses with us, including Bree. By now, she was a professional clinic horse. Being hauled long distances didn't bother her, she ate well, she wasn't upset by stressed horses, and we could trail ride anywhere. She'd discovered that she loved working cattle. I had been in several sticky situations with her, and she was quiet and handled them all with grace. She now met me at the gate; I could clip her bridle path; she could be ridden with a bareback pad and halter at a walk, trot, and canter; and her bushy black mane had grown long and shiny. The light in her eyes had gotten brighter and I was looking forward to spending many years with Bree.

On the day before her first fall, she and I were standing in the middle of a sandy unfenced arena, at the far end from where Mark was teaching and the auditors sat. There was an Appaloosa pony tied to a tree next to where we were working.

I had turned in my saddle to say something to the rider I was working with when I heard a noise from my left that made me look the other way.

It was the pony. He'd slipped out of his halter and, eyes wide and white-rimmed, was on his way toward us at a wild gallop.

I had just enough time to think *This could get interesting* before he was on us. Bree lifted her head from her nap, stepped toward him while pinning her ears, and snaked her neck at him.

The pony whipped off in the opposite direction, and Bree went back to relaxing.

That was the day she saved both of us from what could have been a spectacular wreck. Or at the very least, a large disruption to the clinic going on at the opposite end of the arena.

As the pony was caught, I looked down in wonder at my sleepy mare and thanked her and all the equine gods for the confidence and good judgment of one good horse.

The next day as we groomed and saddled, Bree was restless. I hadn't noticed her acting any differently when we caught her before work that morning, but looking at her, I noticed she wasn't as quiet as the day before. Her eyes had an inward look that she sometimes got when she was worried or uncomfortable.

I ran my hands over her body, checking carefully for any sign of injury. I couldn't find anything. I listened to her abdomen and heard plenty of gurgling. I knelt down and pressed the length of all four of her legs and she stood solid, no signs that anything was wrong.

I stood up and pressed firmly on her back where the saddle would go to make sure she hadn't come up saddle sore. Nothing. I checked her sternum to see if she was sore there. Nothing.

After saddling her and tightening the cinch slowly, I untied her from the trailer and started to lead her toward the arena. Bree reared up and then fell over on her side so quickly that Mark and I only had time to look at her in surprise.

After she stood up, she was breathing heavily, and the expression on her face told me she was just as surprised. Bree had never offered to rear at any time during the year we'd had her; she'd tended to either run or move away.

I unsaddled her, checked her over again, and didn't find anything; I hung a hay net in front of her so she could eat while I worked.

We called a veterinarian out that evening, and I told him what had happened. He listened to her gut again and ran his hands over parts of her body. He did a rectal exam and checked her ovaries. Everything was seemingly normal. He asked me again what happened, and I told him what I could remember.

He walked to her left side and ran his hand down where the girth would go, pressing as he went. When he got halfway down her ribs, right behind her elbow, she flinched and danced away, her tail swishing. He checked again and got the same response.

He guessed that she'd taken a fall in the pasture or gotten kicked and had a possible hairline fracture of one of her ribs where the girth sat. When I tightened the girth, it caused her so much pain she went over backward. He gave her some medicine and recommended eight to twelve weeks off work.

Those eight to twelve weeks turned into three years. In addition to lots of pasture time, Bree had bodywork, acupuncture, and chiropractic. I would pony her on rides or take her hiking. I integrated anti-inflammatory supplements into her diet. She had a herd and she was gaining weight. After a year and a half, I decided to get her out, and slowly saddled her up.

She was nervous, bouncing around on her toes with her ears pinned back. I slowed down even more, breaking up the saddling session over the course of a week.

By the end of the week, she stood saddled. I had a hold of the lead rope this time and hadn't tightened the girth all the way. I asked her to take a few steps toward me, but she reared straight up and fell over backward. As her rehab stretched on and on, I wasn't sure Bree would be able to return to being my clinic horse.

Another year-and-a-half off. Another year-and-a-half of pasture rest and every therapy I could think of for her. I took her out for hikes and we stayed as emotionally close as ever, only this time it felt like I was throwing my heart after false hope. I often wondered if I had the right to get her feeling better only so I could return her to a life that isn't the easiest for a horse.

Was I looking at my selfish tendencies and justifying them, or deluding myself? Whichever it was, I wasn't yet ready to accept that Bree and I were done.

Though each therapy I found and tried helped her a little bit, there was no definite cure. I discovered that I could ride her bareback, but only just. She felt contained, like an uncoiled spring, and I only tried that twice before deciding to give her more time.

Six months later, Mark and I took her on the road again as a way to gather information about her ability to work. At the first clinic on our stop, I got her out each morning, groomed her, and then led her around the arena as I taught. I wanted to be sure that the nervousness she was feeling wasn't some vestigial remembrance of pain. Horses, like people, can often operate on the memory of pain instead of/in addition to actual pain.

After three days of working, she was happy to stand tied at the trailer or to follow me around the arena. By the time we got to our next stop in Florida, I could put the blanket and saddle on her without tightening the girth and she could stand still and didn't look worried

With a break in our schedule, we took the opportunity to go horse camping. It was an ideal time to spend as much time with Bree as I could and see if we could help her through the next step of being saddled. On our first day at the campground, I figured out that if I tightened the girth slowly and let Bree move in a small circle around me, she was okay. No falling over. The whole process took about thirty minutes. Even though this was about twenty-seven minutes longer than it used to take, I didn't care.

I felt a surging sense of relief that my sweet and bold mare was going to make it. That we could, after all, continue working and being together. Bree was doing nicely in a bosal bridle and would go anywhere and do anything she was pointed toward. She responded most of the time, even to new tasks, with a thoughtfulness that was a pleasure to work with. I allowed myself a small dose of hope.

In Florida, we took trail rides in the late morning, moving at a relaxed pace on the sandy trails. I had her on all the supplements I thought were helping her, I continued to get bodywork for her whenever I could, and by the end of our time camping, hope had grown to certainty.

That changed on a warm February day in 2014.

What I remember was that it was another blue-skied Florida day. We were going on a trail ride with friends. I didn't do anything differently with Bree during our saddling-up routine than I had done the half-dozen times we had gone out during our horse camping trip.

I remember my foot going into the stirrup. I remember my right leg swinging over the cantle of the saddle and her hindquarters. I eased down into the saddle. She took a step forward toward Mark, where he sat on his horse, waiting. I gently tilted her nose to the left with my left rein and asked her to take a step back. I remember the soft line of her black mane; it seemed really close.

That's it.

Until I started coming to on the soft sandy ground, with a nice man asking me to wake up. Until I started crying and saying I hadn't paid our health insurance premium yet, so we couldn't go to the hospital. Until I insisted that I be driven because an ambulance was too expensive. Until I realized that the nice man was my husband and his name was Mark.

Once we were in the truck and on the way to the nearest hospital and I was sitting up because I felt nauseous, I looked at my phone to be sure I could still read. I scrolled through my emails to be sure I could bring up a face to match the name.

I think I went to sleep sitting up, because my next memory is of the hospital, and being carried to a bed, and a lot of people making a lot of noise and cutting my clothes off and putting a large needle in my arm and listening to my heart and asking me questions.

SEVEN

THE PINK ROSE CANE

February 5, 2014

I left the hospital with a standard-issue silver crutch tucked under my right arm. We drove to the local drug store to pick up my prescriptions. While we were waiting, I noticed a display of canes. Most of them were the same colors as my right thigh: black, dark blue, angry red. They all somehow screamed an acceptance of a diminished state that I didn't want to stay in permanently.

I dug through the canes and found one at the back, a little dusty, a little forgotten. It was bright pink, with a rose pattern. I drew it out and felt a slow grin spreading across my face. That turned into a broad smile once I discovered that it was adjustable. I clicked it to the right height, put down the crutch I had under my left arm, and set the cane in my right hand.

That was the first clue that my brain injury had rewired my preferences. Before the wreck, I didn't like pink. Or roses. But that day, pink roses seemed to defy the injury. They said that although I needed help walking, I could be cheery while doing it. They said I was not giving in to this injury. They said it's okay to be injured and still appreciate beauty.

The pink rose cane gave others a clue that I couldn't move as they could, but often, I felt like a rock in a stream. People would eddy and rush around me much as springtime Colorado rivers

43

run around boulders in the riverbed when the Rocky Mountain snowpack is melting.

I couldn't rush through anything, though. Mark helped me through the indignity of getting to the toilet. He helped me into the shower and out of it before helping me get dressed, though thankfully since I was living in sweats, tee-shirts, and fleece pullovers, this wasn't as complicated as it might have been. It often occurred to me during this time that your spouse helping you onto the toilet may be a stronger testament of love than his proposal of marriage.

Everything I couldn't do came as a surprise. The list was long and kept getting longer. Since I didn't have any guidance from the hospital doctors other than to stay off the phone, tablet, computer, and television for a month, I experimented with elevating my leg, or not. Icing it, or applying heat. Walking, or lying down because sitting was tortuous. I rebelled and spent an hour on Google trying to figure out how to heal soft-tissue injuries. Apparently, the pain in my swollen leg was taking precedence over my bruised brain.

All of these events happened in the remaining days of our visit with friends. The discoveries of my limitations continued when we needed to travel to our next clinic venue, which was, mercifully, only two hours away. In order to enter and exit our living-quarters trailer, I'd wait for Mark to go down the step first, then wrap my arms around his neck and he would gently lower me to the ground. Getting in and out of our oversized pickup truck also required being lifted.

My sense of everything around me being so fast, however, stopped once I looked at Bree and our other two clinic horses. Though they were grazing and quiet, I was sure I didn't want to be anywhere near them. For the first time in my life when looking at horses, I felt nothing.

I've long been an advocate for taking care of your health and your body as best you can. In 1999, after two years of study, I earned certification in herbalism for people and horses. I then began what was to be a seven-year career in the medical field as a back-office assistant to an ear, nose, and throat doctor (for people, not horses). I experimented with homeopathy and took a Reiki class on a whim. I'd also taken self-defense courses, spent years studying the martial art of aikido, walked, meditated, read spiritual books by the dozens, and educated myself about nutrition and wellness.

Still, I didn't have any idea how to get myself through this injury; two decades of knowledge was locked up, and the keys I had were the wrong size.

I also discovered that I'm absurdly bad about asking for help. Maybe it's because I'm short and think I have something to prove, maybe it's because I'm capable and my belief is that capable people don't need help. Whatever the reasons, I had to let them go if I wanted to get through even a day.

I think most of us are hesitant to ask for help. We love to give help, however. We love to feel useful and needed. What most of us don't like is to feel vulnerable or weak. The good news is that I had a ton of support. The bad news, which turned out to be good news later on, is that I had to face these notions of vulnerability and weakness in the middle of recovering from a head injury and a crushed leg.

Regardless, being helped from the time I woke up to the time I went to bed was not even in the neighborhood of my comfort zone. Deep down, I thought that being vulnerable equated to being a victim, i.e., getting hurt. Then it occurred to me that I was already hurt. Also, deep down, I knew that my unwillingness to be helped was a very old tape, one I'd faced before in therapists' offices. Being unable to do so many things apparently brought those tapes out of hiding, and they played their greatest hits for me. One. More. Time.

Besides old thoughts and pink canes there were other clues that my body and mind were changing. I relished strolling; before the accident, I rarely strolled. Power walking was my gait of choice. Walking slowly and liking it was a new sensation.

I felt like a different person. I could see everything in great detail. I found that each blade of grass was a different shade of green. I saw tiny flowers and felt the variations of the ground under my left foot. I began studying hoof prints to see where a horse was carrying its weight when the hoof landed on the ground.

Everything went so fast! Cars were fast. Most people were even faster. It wasn't just their speech that I could barely follow (though this might've had something to do with the brain injury), or that their actions were speedy. It was as though these things were the by-products of how they felt on the inside. I wondered if this is how we feel to horses: unintelligible and edgy.

Every time I found myself mentally stuck in the mud, I glanced at my pink rose cane and the fog lifted. Somehow, that cheerful and out-of-character cane had come to stand for a more colorful and stable future. It would be a while before that future made itself into the present, however.

Navigating small daily activities I had taken for granted all my life took three times as long, even with my husband's patient help. When I was ready for the day, I would watch as he fed and watered our horses. Through my painkiller haze, I wondered if I would want to go near horses ever again.

I think doubt is common after we're hurt. We question whether it's wise to be involved with whatever it was we were doing when the accident happened. When horses are part of the equation, that thought arises even more aggressively. Humans, after all, have some of the slowest reflexes in the animal kingdom.

You probably know what I am going to say next: horses have among the fastest.

But even knowing this, and knowing that my lifelong love of horses could look vastly different from this point forward, I chose to not worry about it too much. The more important event on my horizon was getting my brain and body back to optimal functioning. Then I could make my choices.

I've discovered that while we may think we are suffering from too much fear, what we are in fact suffering from is an inability to channel it. We are afraid of fear itself, preferring to shove it under that cognitive rug and hope that it goes away. This isn't an accident, it's a feature—an evolutionary design that has kept humans alive for millennia.

If we don't give fear a job, if we can't find ways to engage its message to help us remain safe and alive, it will run wild in our inner house, tearing at the very walls it's supposed to protect. Fear will make its own brand of entertainment. As I well know, when fear entertains itself, whole years of life can disappear.

Before this wreck, I had come off horses a lot. The first thing I always did was get right back on and ride through it.

Except, it turns out, I was never "through it." Now, years later, the dam I'd built against fear had collapsed. The resulting flood changed my interior landscape, and I had to figure out how to channel the emotions. My old strategies weren't working.

I could be okay feeling vulnerable physically. Or even emotionally. But to be at the mercy of vulnerability as a way of living, as an everyday whole-body experience, wasn't something I was ready for.

And we're hardly ever ready for these kinds of events, are we? We prepare, we control, we freak out over things not going our way, and all because (in my case, at least) we think that if we prepare enough, we won't ever be taken by surprise. Even if we are, we've done our time worrying or grieving or being angry, so when the shocks of life hit, we have a savings account of emotions stored up. We can take out an emotion that we've already felt, apply to the situation, and move along.

That's not how it works, although I've tried to make it work for decades.

It makes you wonder, doesn't it? Animals, and horses in particular, don't like surprises either. But because of the way they're made, they can adjust to circumstances most of the time much more quickly than we do. Horses' lives are filled with surprises. As riders, we don't like to be on a horse when it's surprised, since the answer is usually to run first and ask questions later. Yet, we pull them away from their pen and their buddies. We put them in groups of unfamiliar horses, we haul them around in shaky boxes.

When I look at the lives many horses have, I am overwhelmed by how accepting and gracious these creatures are. Sure, some are scared or nervous or worried, but most of the time, if we help them understand what we expect of them, they settle down and try their best.

They bounce back from big changes—being sold from one home to another, being hauled across the country, being badly injured, having a herd-mate leave or die. They will participate in our fast and wild sports with us. They are horses, and they are more. When we are with them, we are more, too.

Riding a horse gives us a chance to touch something that is out of our reach. It is the attraction, the magnetic quality of power coupled with gentleness, and speed combined with beauty.

Every other inanimate thing that humans have created can, through familiarity, take on common qualities. Flying in an airplane or a hot air balloon is fantastic and yet a singular experience. We often lose sight of the fact that we've only been taking to the air with man-made wings since 1903. We're flying!

But we don't feel any enthusiasm coming from the plane itself. The same goes for roller coasters, trains, cars or any other mode of transportation that allows us to move faster than our own legs can carry us. We may feel the poetry when we are in an airplane or on a bicycle, but we feel it by ourselves, not as a shared emotional experience with the plane or balloon or roller coaster.

Riding a horse, or being around horses, is a shared experience. Horses are power sheathed in silky coats. They sweat, they feel a full range of emotions, and they're accepting of humans and all our crazy ideas. They can't be fully controlled. And yet. The thrill of a gallop is a freedom mutually felt. The serenity of grazing is something we can be included in. As we share experiences with our horses, we come to see the world through eyes that aren't blinded by our particular definitions of the world. This world doesn't belong to just us. We share it with every other living creature, plant, and river. Being with a horse allows us to consider other ways of life, and what is important to them.

Three days after the accident, I went to see Dr. Deng, a medical acupuncturist. My body was still sore, and my right leg was black and swollen from my hip to below my knee. Leaning on the pink cane and on pain medication, I limped into her office knowing that this would help, but not looking forward to the process.

Lying on her table after she had finished putting needles into my thigh and head, I shook and cried. At one point she asked me, with sincere puzzlement, "Why are you crying? I'm not doing surgery!" One part of me watched and felt embarrassed for the weepy, trembling woman on the table. There was another part, however, that knew that the crying and shaking were integral to releasing the trauma of the accident. So I let it continue, knowing that it would eventually stop, much as your finger stops hurting once a splinter is out.

That night, I could lift my right foot off the ground a full three inches. I didn't need a pain pill to sleep. Not only do I credit the amazing talents of the acupuncturist, but also my stubbornness in learning about how trauma gets hardwired into our systems. By not reasoning or shaming myself out of the emotions that arose while on Dr. Deng's table, I was able to process a big piece of the accident within a relatively short time. The second treatment was far less emotional but just as beneficial.

During the following days and weeks, I chose therapies that were inside my comfort zone, ones that would be calming and give me immediate relief. Being well acquainted with therapy and its sucky-ness with benefits, I knew I was going to have to face another portion of healing the trauma. I knew what I needed to do. But knowing what you need to do and being willing to do it are two different mindsets.

If I wanted to ride again, my commitment to getting better had to be at least as great as my commitment to horses. It took months and a lot of falling down (and I'm speaking literally, not metaphorically) to reach the place at which I was desperate to try new things.

I had run across Peter Levine and his work almost a decade before, when I was exploring ways to work with anxiety that didn't include pharmaceutical solutions—not that those solutions are wrong. Rather, my interest came from being both nightmarishly sensitive to medications and curious about what lies outside the borders of personal knowledge.

Peter Levine is a psychotherapist and the founder of a particular branch of therapy he calls Somatic Experiencing. He developed this approach after he observed how animals work through trauma and its aftereffects. When applied to the human experience, he noticed that our bodies go through much the same process as any other animal: fight, flee, or freeze; shaking and trembling coming out of shock; and finally, a reset, during which the body and its systems return to normal.

As he helped guide his patients through past traumas—everything from being restrained for childhood shots to car accidents, childhood abuse, and so forth—he noticed that their lives improved through the act of acknowledging and letting their bodies release the life-long trauma they had stored. In some cases, the transformation was miraculous, as in the case of a woman (one of his first clients), who was so intensely anxious that she couldn't leave the house.

In a flash of insight, he asked the woman to imagine that she was running away from a tiger. As she sat and imagined this, her body began to move. Dr. Levine encouraged this movement, asking her to imagine running for her life. Supported by Dr. Levine, she "ran" until her body didn't need to run anymore. After several more sessions, she was a fully functioning, much less anxiety-ridden individual.

The reading I did on the subject confirmed what I was sensing: the traumas I'd experienced had just as much to do with my body as my brain. This is a good news/bad news thing, though. As intelligent folks, we are positive that if we just give something enough thought, if we just figure it out, all will be well. Believe me, I've clung to that notion like it was my last dollar. After all, what could my body possibly have to say that my brain didn't already know?

Turns out, quite a lot. I had to learn how to listen and believe my own body at a level I had never done before. That listening required professional help and practice. And it had nothing to do with horses.

EIGHT

THE CONVERSATION

February 2014

When I landed in the ER there was a flurry of activity. An IV was inserted in my arm, and the medical staff rushed around cutting away my jeans, covering me in a hospital gown, and asking questions. Before the medications took a hold of me, Mark smiled and said, "We can keep Bree as long as you like, but you're never riding her again."

Mark and I don't get in one another's business much, either in our professional or personal lives. We aren't given to issuing one another ultimatums or setting emotional traps. One of the many reasons we do well together is that we recognize we are both adults and can make choices. If the choice seems to be questionable, there's a discussion about it before making a final decision. And then it's accepted.

So when he told me I wasn't riding Bree ever again, I took it seriously. I remember he was sitting to my left, near me but out of the way of the medical staff. The expression on his face was soft, but the tone in his voice was firm. I also knew somewhere in the back of my bruised brain that he'd been shaken by the accident, which he'd watched from start to finish from only a few feet away. It was over and done in less than two seconds; he didn't even have time to dismount before Bree was scrambling up, leaving me lying unconscious and staring into a sky I didn't see.

Lying on the hard hospital bed, feeling like the inside of my head was a steel sieve and my leg a black-and-blue balloon, I knew he was right.

Once we left Florida on our way to the next clinic stop in Texas, we chatted about our options for Bree. We could keep her and, once home, take her to Colorado State University vet school for a workup to find out what caused her to collapse. We could keep her and not take her to CSU because to all appearances, she was healthy and thriving. We could find a home for her where we were sure she wouldn't ever be ridden. Of these options, the last one felt the worst.

If we kept Bree, she would spend seven months of her life in a paddock at our barn and we would see her once every month or so while we were home. The other five months she would be on pasture with other horses. I was looking at the quality of her life and doing my best to take her point of view into consideration.

Letting her hang out in our herd, while viable, wasn't a very rich life. Being shuffled back and forth from barn to pasture with very little interaction with the people she had grown to appreciate seemed almost cruel.

We could take Bree to CSU, spend thousands of dollars, and still not have an answer. We'd had her checked over by vets multiple times, including after she fell with me, and the results were always the same: she was a healthy mare. Healthy, except for the fact that she'd rear up and fall over backward when there was pressure in her girth area. The scary part was that she couldn't seem to control herself. The reality was that even if we had answers, the result was the same: she couldn't be ridden anymore.

Whatever option we decided on, her life was going to be one that included her not being ridden, ever, under any circumstances.

Ignoring the neurologist's strict orders that I avoid looking at my phone or tablet, I emailed our friend Allyson DeCanio, who runs the Pegasus Project horse rescue in Texas with her husband Mike. I thought that since we were on our way to give a clinic there, she might have some ideas about Bree's options. I asked if she knew of anyone who would like a really nice mare as a companion horse. Truthfully, I didn't think there was much of a chance, because homes for rescue horses are far fewer than the number of horses who need them.

I didn't hear anything for a half hour. Then I got an email from Allyson saying that she'd found a potential place for Bree with a lady named Debbie. An hour before Allyson got my email, she'd heard from Debbie, who said she would love to foster another Arabian mare as a companion to the one she was already fostering.

I'm a big believer that most things work out if we give them a chance, but this felt like fate was resetting the playing field. Bree could have a home with another horse and a human who had zero interest in riding. Debbie liked Arabians, and she was particularly thrilled that Bree was a bay because the mare she had was also a bay. We had Bree with us and we were landing at the Pegasus Project as our next clinic stop.

When things click in to place so easily, I know there is some force afoot. I felt that this force was offering an opportunity, a possible solution that would work out well for both me and Bree. In the same message, Allyson said that not only did Debbie have a bay Arabian mare, but also, chickens, a mini-mule, dogs, and cats. Plus, Bree would have constant turnout.

It meant saying a difficult goodbye to Bree. We'd learned from each other and looked out for each other. Though I'd started dozens of colts and, later, older horses, she was the first horse with whom I'd tested my knowledge of the principles that Mark and I strive to live by. She was quiet, confident, sweet, and kind. She was my clinic horse, a partner, and also a source of joy for me.

Even after this accident, I didn't feel anything but gratitude for her. I realized that I couldn't see her spending the next ten to fifteen years being shuffled back and forth from barn to pasture, being physically taken care of but not having people around very much.

The morning after we arrived at the clinic venue, Debbie showed up to meet Bree. I felt like a monster, considering giving away my mare. I felt relief that Bree would have someone doting on her. I felt the weight of grief that our relationship had reached this point and that I wouldn't ever work with her again. But I liked the way Debbie approached Bree and touched her, and the way Bree, people-lover that she had become, reached back to Debbie. I hobbled out of the pen to give them some space.

As I limped away from them, I thought about my belief that horses have an intrinsic worth in and of themselves. Horses don't have to be ridden in order to be valued, and these days, there are far more options for horses who can't be ridden, such as becoming therapy horses or companion animals.

While I watched Debbie and Bree get to know each other, it became very clear to me that Bree would have a far more interesting and people-centered life somewhere else. I trusted Allyson's judgment and her process for finding foster homes, and if ever Debbie couldn't keep Bree, she could go back to Pegasus or return to us.

It was a best-case scenario, so when Debbie closed the gate to Bree's pen and came over to talk to me, I blurted out, "I think she'd be happy with you." Debbie smiled and said she would be happy to have Bree.

Debbie left after letting us know that she would be back the next day with her trailer to take Bree to her new home.

That evening, when the only sounds were birds singing in the moonlight and horses chewing hay, I limped over to Bree's pen. I wanted to say goodbye but found I couldn't say the word. Instead, I thanked her for all she had taught me. I let her know that while this next part of her life would be very different and confusing, she would be taken care of. Letting her know that what had happened was an accident and there weren't any hard feelings. I poured my heart out to my little brave mare in ways I wasn't aware that I needed.

I don't know if horses understand our words. But I do know deep in my bones that they understand something. Intent? Energy? Whatever it is and however they know it, Bree knew too. She stopped eating and stood by me with her head at eye level, breathing gently and closing her eyes. I hugged her around her neck. She leaned into me and exhaled.

Forgiveness is hard won. Forgiveness for Bree wasn't needed at this point; she was a horse who was in pain, expressing that pain the only way she could.

But for myself? As Bree resumed her hay-chewing, I felt that I needed forgiveness for not seeing the signs that she was unfit to ride. If she had the kind of pain that would literally drop her to the ground, what possessed me to believe I could help her through that? Pride? A false sense of security? I took a long, hard look at whether I'd started to think that I was any kind of an expert when it came to horses. The question "Who do you think you are?" was exploding like fireworks inside my head.

I began to think that another profession sounded pretty great. The perks were obvious: no sitting in a truck for upwards of ten hours a day as we hauled to our next clinic. No late nights and very early mornings. No dragging horses around the country in all kinds of weather and subjecting them to so much that is outside of what they are built for. No wondering if we were going to make the long ends of our bills meet the short ends of our self-employed paychecks. Never being troubled by the worry that the information I was trying to share with people in our lessons was coming across the way I intended it. No more being away from our mountain home for weeks and months at a stretch. No more.

As I left Bree's pen, I realized that my brain felt like it was slipping gears and no fresh thoughts arose about a new career. At least, not ones I needed to pay attention to in the present. As my cane hit the soft ground with each step, I reminded myself that there was enough going on with my brain and body that I didn't need to solve the puzzle of whether or not to keep working with horses. The ease with which I sank into that truth let me know that I had time, and in that time, I could work with things as and if they arose.

In the following days, as Debbie settled Bree in her new home, I heard about "spa" treatments—Bree was being bathed and groomed and fussed over. She and the other Arab mare were constant companions, eating from the same hay pile, trotting around and flipping their heads as though they had been studying with an equine choreographer.

It helped to hear that she was content and enjoying her new home. Debbie said she found Bree a delight to have around.

I couldn't have agreed more.

NINE

AN UNRULY
TOMATO PLANT

In the summer, I like to keep a few pots of herbs and vegetables on our south-facing porch. The growing season is short where we live, and between the weather and the deer who like the same herbs and vegetables I do, growing food in pots means the odds that I'll be able to enjoy the herbs and vegetables go up.

When we're home, I check on the tomato plant at different times of the day. I make sure the morning sun reaches it first, and give it water. In the afternoon, I smell the tangy leaves and think of my Nana, who grew tomatoes the respectable way: in the dirt, in a good old-fashioned southern garden. In the evening, I water it again and admire how some tomatoes have grown in size and others are in various stages of going from green to red.

The leaves feel scratchy. The stalks refuse to be contained in their bamboo supports. I don't know much about gardening, but I've discovered that tomatoes are a most unruly plant. I'm sure there are other unruly food sources out there, but the potted tomato plant on our summer porch is my only frame of reference.

During my care of the tomatoes, I've often thought that a fear of returning to being with horses is unruly, too. Fear likes to visit unannounced and horses don't conform to our rules. They are, for all their domestic ways, quite wild. They can seem unruly to us, but what they are doing is following their own true nature.

It occurs to me that we allow our fear to be like that tomato plant. Despite constant tending, or maybe because of it, it grows wild and unruly even when we try to contain it. Fear is being true to its nature as well.

All of our emotions have a job to do. They serve a purpose—positive or negative—whether we like it or not. Though there have been times I wished I were more like Spock from Star Trek, when I think of the times I've felt any intense emotion, I realize that as unruly as those emotions are, they come and go. Nothing is permanent, even if it feels like it is. I often remember what Pema Chödrön says: "You are the sky. Everything else—it's just the weather."

The sun rises and sets and each new day is different. My tomato plant thrives and ripens and then withers as the days grow shorter and colder. I mourn this, the fall into the darker spaces of winter. I am sorry to see the flowers go from green and colorful to brown and brittle. Sad to put all the cheery pots away until the next spring. As often as I've thought about the seasons and the cycles of life that we all participate in, it doesn't lessen my grief to see the flowers' colors drain away. But it does do wonders for my learning the constant lesson of acceptance of the passage of time, and the cyclical nature of life.

Our fear and anxiety around horses thrive in the sunlight of obsession. The more we focus on the fear, the bigger it seems to be. It's like doing shadow animals in the light of a candle; the shadows our hands cast are much bigger than our actual hands.

Our fear doesn't need tending or befriending, but our confidence does.

After any kind of accident with a horse, fear feels vast and insurmountable. After my accident with Bree, I naturally attached that fear to everything that was involved with it: the horse, the soft line of a black mane, the dirt, the saddle, the state of Florida. I wanted nothing to do with any of it. I hoped that shunning my fear in a cold blast of emotional winter would cause it to wither and die.

But it didn't. For all my ardent wishes that I wouldn't be afraid around horses, for all my wanting to "move forward," or "get over it," nothing changed until I owned the fear, and then figured out ways to tend to my confidence.

Just like my little tomato plant, I put my confidence somewhere safe. I protected it and counted every fruit as it burst into life. I made sure the soil was nourished and kept moist. I was mindful to avoid setting it out in conditions that might cause it to be knocked over.

What did this mean on a practical level? I decided to only put myself in the proximity of our own herd or horses I was familiar with. I chose practices that had a noticeable effect on my state of mind (*numero uno* is putting attention on my breath) and that I could do anywhere. I started a brain-supplement regimen and a way of eating to help my brain heal.

Whatever you want to do, there are creative ways you can do that thing. It may not look like anything else anyone else is doing, but so what? It's your life, and your peace of mind that's important. The fruit of ripened confidence is about the most delicious thing there is.

I've discovered that robust confidence includes both the brain and the body. Once I was able to do things with my body and started to gain strength and feel less pain, my thoughts about horses began to shift from a great big NO to a softer maybe.

But if we only heal physically, most of us will begin to notice a vague sense of discomfort when we think about riding. Or we will procrastinate about being around our horse. Maybe say we really like riding only on the trail, or only in the arena, or only at one o'clock on Wednesday afternoons. We may buy and sell a lot of different horses, trying to find one that's "right," but never doing so.

We may choose to get away from horses altogether. We may also choose to stay with horses, but do activities with them that are different than what we did before. These are all valid paths.

Most of us don't know that something's amiss, or that we need help to continue doing what we once loved. Fear is a sneaky thief in this regard; arriving sometimes in slippers, sometimes with a club.

I get that fear's goal is to keep us safe. The sound of fear's arrival may differ, but the announcement is always the same: don't do this, don't do that, and certainly don't do the other. Fear's message often can be that we need to be protected, and feeling protected is what fosters a sense of safety. A sense of security is integral to how we feel about not only horses, but being out in the world. If we aren't careful, though, our fear can tell us that the only place we are safe is in bed, or in our house. But definitely not anywhere near a horse ever again. Fear has a job, and it also has limitations. We need to be aware of both sides of its nature, and not spend so much time in its company that it smothers our innate sense of curiosity or our innate joy in a horse-centered life.

It's also important to remember that it doesn't take coming off a horse to register something as an injury, or a shock. Whether it's the threat of a bite or kick, or an actual bite or kick, we retain some part of that experience, coupled with feelings of danger and fear. It's been shown that whether you witness a wedding or a death, you may experience the sensations as though it has happened to you. See enough accidents with horses and if you have your own history of accidents, your brain and body will do an excellent job of convincing you that it's better to go back inside and watch television.

But TVs don't have sweet hay breath. They don't tickle your

ear with their whiskers, and they certainly don't greet you with low rumbly nickers. Sitting on the couch, waiting for the storm of your horse-fear to pass, is akin to chewing your food but not swallowing it. You might feel temporarily satisfied by the flavor, but there isn't any nourishment. We can't live like that.

Though fear and lack of confidence with horses may feel unruly right now, there are small steps you can take to help yourself feel better. Whether friends, trainers, family members, or therapists, there are people who can help you tend your confidence and show you ways to let your fear wither to manageable proportions. While I wholeheartedly applaud caution and common sense when it comes to being around horses, I also applaud being able to let our happiness with horses outshine our fear. It's time to lengthen our days and bask in the sunlight of ease and confidence.

TEN

BREATH AS A BRIDGE

Our breath acts as a bridge between two shores: one, the coastline of calmness and presence and the other, of anxiety and worry. The way we breathe determines which of these shores we inhabit. For many years, I chose to pound the sands of anxiety. I still go there—you know, just to be sure I haven't forgotten the way. However, those visits are brief and I no longer feel lost. Breathing is both my bridge and my path.

Breathing can run on its own or we can consciously influence it. We usually don't think about breathing when we sleep or when we are focused on a task. Ideally, we consciously think about it when we are upset, angry, or meditating. Our breath is so familiar to us, so basic and intimate and woven into who we are and how we do things that paying attention to it often feels like trying to watch the digestive process, which also takes care of itself without our focus or attention.

Over time, we may unconsciously slip into the mindset of, "Why make the effort when it's going to happen anyway?"

If we don't pay attention to the breath when we're anxious, it will often trap us in a place of feeling afraid and overwhelmed. This is because when we are fighting or running from danger, or when we feel threatened, we breathe shallowly. Our body goes through a very rapid process: blood is shunted to the muscles, digestion slows, and the part of our brain evolved for survival lights up. Our muscles tense for the effort they will need to run or fight, and chemicals flood our nervous system, chemicals that some modern-day drugs mimic.

In other words, if we make a habit of breathing shallowly, we are building our house on the edge of a cliff and crossing our fingers against landslides. We wake up, we eat, we work, we pursue our interests, and we certainly ride, as though at any moment, a lion is going to burst from the bushes.

In light of this, isn't it odd that we wonder why our horse "spooks at nothing"? Many things a horse will or will not do with us are influenced by the way we breathe. Choppy transitions? The rider is holding their breath. Lack of scope over a jump? The rider is holding their breath. The horse stands with its head up in the air, on alert? Guess what isn't happening. While you're around your horse, are you breathing slowly and deeply?

Now certainly, there are other reasons for equine discomfort, ones with which most of us are well acquainted: saddle fit, pain, unbalanced feet or teeth. Here's the thing, though: when you're not breathing well, you and your horse will have a very difficult time achieving your mutual best together. You can have a great-fitting saddle, the best farrier, a fantastic dentist, a skilled bodyworker, and a great trainer. Without effective breathing, all these things will only get you, and your horse, so far.

Have you ever been in a restaurant and heard the crash of dishes hitting the floor? Or seen the brake lights of the car in front of you suddenly flash on? When someone unexpectedly walks up beside or behind you, what is your response? Most people will startle and momentarily hold their breath. This is because they were taking shallow, quick breaths in the first place.

If we are living our lives on the edge of a metaphorical cliff, an accident or injury can leave us feeling like we are caught in a landslide with only the deep blue ocean below us.

When we focus on keeping both our inhalations and exhalations long, slow, and deep, we can help ourselves feel (and be) calmer. Slower. Less frantic. When I could do nothing else, breathing in deeply enough to feel my ribs stretch and expand, and breathing out until every last bit of oxygen had left my lungs, put me in a state of absolute presence, and sometimes a welcome, albeit brief, tranquility.

Although we can't feel it, slow and deep breathing facilitates the movement of our internal organs. When we breathe deeply, our diaphragm (the muscular partition that separates our heart and lungs from our stomach and intestines) rises and falls. As it rises and falls, it creates space, then fills space. Since we have organs both above and below this space, those organs move to accommodate the diaphragm's movement. (Interestingly, we have a second diaphragm in our pelvis, but for our purposes here we will focus on the one that is closest to our lungs.)

If you've ever watched the ocean, you will have noticed that the waves roll in and out at a certain rhythm. This rhythm may alter if there's been a storm but the waves always come in and go out again. Every minute, every day, every week, every month, every year. Waves rise and fall, advance and retreat. If we quiet our minds and bring our attention to the water's pattern, we might find that our breathing gradually synchronizes with the rhythm of the waves.

You don't, however, need to go to the ocean to feel as though you're on the beach. A breath that first expands your ribcage and then fills your chest has the potential to induce the same sense of calm. When your internal organs are moving, when your diaphragm, much like the ocean waves, is doing its job of rising and falling, your body will relax. You will feel less anxious, and your thoughts will slow down.

Let's try this: put your right hand under your right collarbone and your left hand over the bottom left of your ribcage.

Take a breath. Which hand moved? Did your right hand rise and fall and your left hand remain still? If so, the way you're breathing is the way you breathe when you're close to or in an anxiety/fear state. By extension, this means that when you go out to your horse, where fear and/or anxiety may arise, it's going to feel more intense because your body is set up for tension by this breathing pattern.

Now, move your right hand down so it is opposite your left, bracketing your ribcage. Can you breathe deeply enough to cause both hands to move? This is the type of breathing that sets us up to feel calmer and more relaxed. It's the way we need to breathe most of the day because when we get to our horse (where we are going to feel more nervous), we want to give our body a way to turn off the alarm system. Breathing slowly and deeply is the key.

Another way to think about breathing effectively is as though you are filling your lungs with air the way you would fill a glass with water. When we pour water into the glass, it doesn't start at the top and hover there. It flows to the bottom of the glass and fills up to the top. So it is with air and our lungs: we are designed so that air goes to the bottom first (ribcage breaths) and inflates our chest last.

Feeling better, in general, is a great motivation to become more mindful about how you breathe. Another motivating reason is that for horses, long, slow breaths signal a calm state at an instinctually powerful level. Conversely, breath-holding (theirs or ours) signals them to be on the alert, to allow the other senses to take over and let them know if the danger is worth running away from. I don't know about you, but I would prefer my horse to feel as though we're walking in a park, not being chased by lions.

ELEVEN
ALLY FINDS US

March 2014

After Bree went to her new home with Debbie, we continued working at the Pegasus Project. One day as I limped by the arena, leaning heavily on my cane, I heard Mark saying, "This is a really nice horse. She'd make an excellent horse for someone small. You know, a short woman. What a nice horse." Eventually, I noticed that he was looking at me and smiling, and realized he was trying to get me to see the Quarter Horse mare trotting in the arena.

Built compactly, she was attentive to her rider; I saw no worry as she walked, trotted, and cantered easily. I liked the kind look in her eye. Her rider, one of the trainers at the facility, said she had been restarted three weeks earlier. Mark mentioned that it looked like somewhere in her past, she'd had a lot of training.

After they were done with their session, I went over to the pen she was in and leaned on the panels, looking at her. Her eyes were deep, quiet, and soft. She ambled over to me and sniffed the arm that was leaning on the fence. I stroked her nose. She followed me to the end of her pen, and as I limped away, I glanced back over my shoulder and saw that she was still watching me.

The next day, I asked if I could get her out and groom her. I hadn't planned on getting another horse so soon, thinking that perhaps I would need time for the right one to find me. I knew that horses are experts at finding the right people for them, and I was prepared to let myself heal, and wait.

But before the day was done, we had adopted her and put her in the pen with our horses. I named her Ally, after my friend Allyson, who had not only orchestrated Bree's adoption but two years prior, had rescued this mare and nursed her back to health so she could find us exactly when we needed her.

Only two weeks out from a head injury, I didn't fully trust myself to make sound decisions. I could barely decide how to dress in the morning, much less if a new horse was right for me or not. But I did trust Mark's judgment, and so Ally and I started to get to know one another.

When I went to the pen the next day, she walked over and stood quietly, taking breaths that were slow and deep. I was glad one of us could. I leaned my cane against the fence so I could put her halter on. After that, I took my cane, and led her through the opening, fumbling with the gate and lead rope and cane. Ally waited while I figured it out, then walked through the gate, waiting while I closed it.

I turned slowly and began to walk to the area where I would groom her. I had the pink cane in my right hand and the lead rope in my left. Ally watched me walk, and then came with me, matching exactly my pace and staying behind and beside me. By the time we got to the fence where I would tie her, I knew we had found each other.

After weeks of pain and worry, the simple act of haltering and leading a kind and quiet horse were the crucial bits of information I needed. Could I do these seemingly small things with less fear? Could I do them at all? The happiness I felt when those answers were both yes was as pain-relieving as any medication.

Whether it's the horse you had an accident with or another, these first interactions are crucial to your ability to continue building your confidence. If you need a trusted friend or instructor to help you, definitely do so. If you choose to start by yourself, take it slowly. It could be that just walking to catch your horse feels stressful.

Going slowly and being with horses for short intervals will help your confidence start to grow again. It may be that watching your horse in his paddock or stall will be enough to begin with. Putting a halter on and taking it off may be the next step. Then leading, then grooming, until one day, you can do all of this without worry or concern.

Having small, reachable goals is so much kinder than having goals that feel terrifying. Or trying to reach someone else's goals. Figuring out what we can do while still being able to breathe and feel good isn't difficult; all that's needed is a bit of self-awareness and a bit of time. I think horse people are generally a self-aware bunch. Otherwise, how could we successfully ride such big, fast animals?

Adding some outside support from a spouse, family member, friend, or a trainer you feel comfortable with and figuring out how to nurture your confidence can be an easier path than you imagine. If you're anything like me, on your own, it's way too easy to imagine a whole mess of wrongness.

The day Ally and I met and interacted for the first time was monumental. In my life, I've had many amazing and intensely joyful experiences with horses. That first day with Ally was as large as getting a ribbon at a show or moving cattle across the Arizona plains from sunup to sundown. Walking and leading and grooming reignited the light inside me and started me on yet another path of firsts, this time with a different horse.

I am also grateful to have received such excellent support and kindness from Mark as well as family and friends. One piece of information that landed in a big way during our time in Texas came from our friend Rosalie, who had been a large-animal veterinarian for many years.

After I'd shared a brief history of what led up to Bree falling with me, she asked what I thought it was that made Bree collapse. I responded that several vets hadn't found anything and, except for a possible pasture accident three years prior, I was at a loss.

She thought about that for a moment, then told me about an experience she'd had while in vet school.

A pony was brought to be euthanized and then donated to the vet school for a necropsy. The pony was known for violent behavior and wouldn't be ridden. No matter how they bullied or coerced him, a saddle was out of the question. As he got older, the behavior became worse, and the owners decided that euthanization was their only alternative.

During the necropsy, after exposing the ribcage, the students noted that the muscles and bones looked normal on the outside. But once the sternum was separated and they opened the ribcage, they saw that the pony had a large mass on one of his ribs, in the area over which a girth would have been tightened.

Rosalie also gave me the name of a vet who had done years of research on sleep deprivation in horses. I thanked her for this information and limped back to the trailer to lie down.

The more I thought about it, the more I realized that Bree had signs that would fit both instances. I also realized that the mystery may never be solved. Even if it was, she was no longer my clinic horse, or even a riding horse. She was no longer mine at all.

I began to educate myself on what's known about sleep patterns in horses. I realized that I had never actually seen Bree lying down and sleeping. She never had grass or shavings on one side of her body. I wondered how long that had been going on, and why I hadn't noticed it.

We see hundreds of horses and riders each year. We help people figure out ways to communicate better, and when their horse might need extra help in the form of vet care or bodywork. We are the people other people come to for guidance.

Realizing that I'd apparently overlooked something this basic brought on a flood of doubt about my skills as a horse person. It felt like a whole crushed leg's worth of shame and resignation. Later, on our way home to Colorado with Ally and our other horses, I recognized that between the rock of fear and the hard place of that doubt, my desire to work as a horse trainer and instructor was on shaky ground. Although being with Ally had brought a surge of reassurance, sitting in a truck for two days with the pain in my leg overriding the beauty of the countryside blossoming into spring gave my mind a chance to run rampant, and not in a good way.

It would be so much easier to be a librarian, I thought, and so much more suited to my introverted nature. Books don't kill people and books don't kick or bite or suffer. I could bask in silence, I could micro-organize and be paid for it. My days would be spent with books and quiet and orderliness and reading.

I didn't have any idea what my life was going to look like, either in the near future or a year away. Even the pain in my leg wasn't a match for the pain in my mind. I was feeling low and pitiful, and didn't like the feeling one bit.

TWELVE
HOMECOMING

April 2014

The first morning after we got home, the burning question I woke up with was, will I ever be able to—or want to—ride again? Mark helped me out to the paddock behind our house, where we haltered our oldest horse, Tuff. He was first Mark's clinic horse and has carried riders of all experience levels for many years. Tuff and I'd had many adventures, and I trusted him, quite literally, with my life.

Mark boosted me onto Tuff's broad back and I waited for the panic to set in; I had mentally prepared myself for the possibility of falling apart. Instead, what I felt was a rush of relief and a flood of joy. Tuff carried me for fewer than five minutes, but it was enough to show me that if I was mindful about how I returned to working with horses, joy was possible.

Possibilities, I discovered that day, are far more potent than fear.

After questioning the direction of my life and whether it would have horses in it, I was surprised by the peace I felt as I sat bareback on Tuff. As we walked near the forest that surrounds our house, I realized that at some point, I could potentially feel content and relaxed with horses once again. My deep love for them hadn't been taken away, just shaken. The mystery of their movements, the beauty of the wind through their manes, their wild-grass smell, their sounds, and their liquid and gentle eyes still enchanted me. Though it might take me years, I knew that with help, I could find my way back.

Feeling encouraged and a little bit wild after my ride, I asked Mark to take me to our barn on the other side of town so I could try riding Ally. Just the thought made my heart speed up, and the familiar sensation of falling into a pit started bubbling up through my belly.

Once at the barn, Mark brought Ally out of the herd and stood by as I hobbled around her, running a brush over her slick bay coat. I put a puffy bareback pad on her, found a bridle, and, after some deep breathing, had Mark boost me up on her. I inadvertently kicked her with my injured right leg several times while trying to swing it over her back. Once I settled down, it felt like I was riding with a large, round stone underneath my throbbing thigh. I kept breathing, and Ally never moved. She barely raised her head.

After several minutes, I let Mark know it was okay to let go of her bridle, then sat a few moments before asking her to move forward. She turned her head to the left, her liquid eye turning up to me, and I swore I heard her ask, "Are you sure about that?" I breathed, and asked again, and she turned her head toward me again. She then straightened out and took one very slow, very small step, stopped, and turned her head to look at me again.

At that moment, I discovered what a great antidote laughter is to fear. I also knew, without a doubt, that Ally and I were going to be perfect for each other. I silently agreed that one step was indeed enough, and called it a day.

After that, I didn't ride again while we were home. The injury was still painful and my leg was still swollen. I'd been told that sometimes, a soft-tissue injury will take longer to heal than a broken bone, and I was finding this to be annoyingly accurate.

Then in April, we headed out to clinics in California, where I started riding Ally for brief periods, which was about all my leg could handle. As it turned out, this was an excellent benefit for my nervous system too. By taking slow, small rides, I was beginning to rebuild my confidence, and doing it more solidly than when following my previous strategy, which was basically to get on a horse and attempt to ride through the fear. Ally was the quiet to my frantic, the calm to my nervousness. I started to allow a little bit of trust to creep between me and my fear.

I was fortunate that Mark found Ally for me, as I'm not sure I could've ridden Bree again even if she'd been rideable. But what if you want to keep the horse you had an accident with? What if, despite your fear, you wish to someday be around that same horse, ride again, and perhaps pursue the activities you were doing before?

One way to start is with a thorough assessment of your horse. This will not only give you more information but also, a bit more peace of mind. Knowledge is not only power but a great reassurance when you're unsure.

Some ways you might go about gathering information about your horse include:

- a full vet checkup;

- soft-tissue bodywork by a certified equine bodyworker;

- a consult with a certified equine chiropractor;

- a consult with a farrier (or a second opinion to confirm what you've been told or think you know);

- a consult with an equine dentist to be sure your horse's teeth are balanced and not cracked or painful; and

- a consult with a knowledgeable trainer to make sure your horse's tack fits correctly.

After you've gathered information about your horse, you can then begin to re-engage. The pace is completely up to you. Some people might want to groom for a month before getting back on. Some may feel good about longeing their horses, some may want to take them for walks or hikes; I am a big fan of this too. Some may want to call their trainer, saddle up, and go for it. Or at least saddle up.

If you have a friend who has a quiet horse, you might ask if you could spend some time being around their horse, or even riding with them. You could also ask someone else—a trainer or an experienced friend—to work with your horse. Whatever you decide to do, it's beneficial to have someone you trust by your side to reassure you and double-check your choices.

It's best if the person you choose for this role doesn't have an agenda about you getting back on your horse. If you need to get on and then get right off and go for a brisk walk, you want someone who will walk with you rather than press you to stay mounted longer. You are the architect of these plans, so to speak, and you are also the best person to know when you can ride longer or go faster.

Whatever your choice, what we're discussing here is doing what you feel is appropriate and Slowing. Way. Down. We're sometimes in a rush to prove that we aren't afraid even while the deepest part of our brain is actually screaming, "Get off this big, flighty creature! Right Now!" We rush to prove we're capable horse people, that we aren't failures. We can be so focused on what are basically ego issues that we get ourselves in trouble and worry our horses. Less worry for both you and your horse is what this is all about.

Less worry was what I was aiming for, too. The voices in my head told me that the sooner I got back on, the sooner I would feel better. The sooner I conquered my fear . . . got back out on the trail . . . could ride a walk, trot, and canter, the sooner I would be a better rider. The sooner I could justify my existence as a horse trainer and instructor. The voices in my head said it could all be done if I was "brave enough" to get back on a horse. Some days, the litany was endless.

Fortunately, I was able to recognize that the voices sounded suspiciously like those of some of my past riding instructors, who didn't know any better. Understanding that didn't stop the voices, but it did take away their power to make choices for me.

I've seen hundreds of people who are holding on to trauma but would like to ride without it as their companion. The other interesting phenomenon I've witnessed is that while many people wish to feel better, very few actually pursue it with a plan or commitment. They are committed to their horses and committed to their friends' or trainers' opinions of them, but haven't yet extended that commitment to themselves.

To be honest, I was in that category until this accident. The clarity that found me in the middle of a traumatic brain injury startled me out of complacence. It was evident that if I didn't do something to heal internally, my life was going to look and feel much different.

Since I couldn't teach or ride, I had time to think about whether a life with horses was still for me. Yes, I had dreamt of it since I was a child. Yes, it was the way I loved to make a living and a life. But, as mentioned earlier, I also made room for the possibility that it was perhaps time to do something else.

Then, my ride on Tuff showed me that my heart was still smitten with horses. It wasn't yet time to walk away from them, or from teaching or riding. It was, however, clear that it was time to start moving away from the fear I'd accumulated. After that, it was only a matter of logic: if I wanted to continue working with horses and people, I had to feel better and regain confidence. Therefore, I was going to need help. A lot of it.

So much support is available to us at any given moment, but we need to ask for it. Before you mutter "Easy for you to say," let me confess that my inner control freak is alive and has a clean bill of health. It took a head injury and not having full use of my right leg for almost a year before I tried something that was far more painful than my injuries: admitting I needed help.

But it's a lot easier these days. Helping others has always been my comfort zone, and a route to happiness. As I healed my way through this accident, however, it dawned on me that acceptance is a much softer bed than denial, even when there is mental and physical pain. I realized I could also be happy by letting others feel good about being of assistance.

THIRTEEN
A CURIOUS MIND

As one month turned into two, it dawned on me that I no longer felt irritated or rushed. The litany of monotonous self-judgment was silent. And despite being in more physical pain than I had ever experienced, I felt a deep sense of calm.

Perhaps there's a psychological theory behind this, but at the time, it didn't matter to me. Not much did. It wasn't as though I didn't care, because I still cared about what I had cared about before. I still felt invested in those I loved, human and animal. It was more that I felt a deep and abiding sense of well-being that nothing in my day could shake loose.

Resentment disappeared. Gratitude took its place.

All injuries change us, brain injuries especially so. I am grateful that in spite of a few glitches—some short-term memory loss and losing words when I get tired or stressed—who I am and how I think have remained mostly unchanged. I have experienced what it feels like to live in a state of peace. I know it's possible to return to that state, even though these days, my brain is firing on all cylinders, including hamster-wheel thinking, jumping to conclusions, and the specific mischief of anxiety.

However, none of that surface stuff can take away the knowledge and experience of feeling deeply at ease with myself and life. I know that if I support my body and choose that peace, I can get close to it, if not right down in the middle of it.

Since I'm fundamentally a curious person (or fundamentally averse to feeling out of control—the line is fine between the two), when I'm experiencing something that isn't comfortable, I go hunting for a way to shift it.

Some time ago, I came across a theory called "the triune brain," which is based on the idea that the brain evolved in three different stages. While the term isn't used by many mental health professionals, it has an elegant simplicity, a way to explain why thinking your way out of trauma is often unsuccessful. Peter Levine refers to this theory, which was first proposed by Paul MacLean, and I would like to share it here.

The first and oldest part is called the reptilian brain. It's mostly concerned with essential functions such as regulation of heartbeat, body temperature, and breathing.

Next is the paleomammalian (or limbic) brain, home to the limbic system. The functions of this system arose early in mammalian evolution and are responsible not only for emotion but also, the motivation to reproduce and raise offspring. Additionally, this area is involved in value judgments and their influence on our behavior.

The last part of the human brain to evolve is the neomammalian (or neocortex). This is where more advanced functions such as planning, impulse control, abstraction, and perception reside.

Here's the key: we cannot use one part of our brain (the neocortex, the newest) to talk, reason, or manipulate another part (the reptilian brain, the oldest) out of fear and terror. It's as though the brain is Asia: one continent, many languages.

When you remember a horse accident, does your breathing stay long, slow, and deep or does it become shallow, or stop? Does your heart rate increase? These sensations are signals that your survival systems are coming online. The brain cannot tell the difference between something actually happening and something that you are remembering or visualizing happening. Once the brain goes on alert, the body is quick to follow.

This is what I mean about one part of the brain not convincing the other part. When there is a choice between survival and thinking, survival will win every time. And much like horses, if we are fearful, we cannot be curious, and curiosity is part of what helps fear dissipate.

Give this a shot: can you remember a subject in school that was sheer torture for you?

My personal rack of awfulness was math. After second grade, nothing beyond addition computed. I couldn't get it, I didn't understand, and the more I didn't get it, the more frustrated I got. I remember my father trying to help me, and my uncle, too. Seeing their frustration only made my dismay worse. I don't know how I scraped through, but by the time I reached Mr. B's algebra class in eighth grade, I was close to giving up. Only the horror of a bad report card kept me trying.

Mr. B. was different. He was funny and engaging, and really liked the subject he taught. That in itself caused me to wonder about him. How could someone enjoy math?! This was a mystery that not only aroused my curiosity but needed answers. At the end of class, he would often trot out the same joke: "Go home and tell your parents you learned about LCD today." To this day, I know he meant the Lowest Common Denominator. (I've forgotten what that is or what it does, but I do at least know what LCD stands for.)

That year, I started paying attention and doing the homework. I joined the whole class in laughter, and math was almost as enjoyable as English. My anxiety went down—though never away—and my learning went up. I got my first B in math that year, and when ninth grade started, I wasn't as scared of math as I had been. I remember feeling that with help, I could figure it out.

When you were in school feeling tortured by, let's say, math, was there a moment that helped you shift your gears from fear and frustration into curiosity? Do you remember the moment when you could look at an assignment or do the homework and not feel as though you wanted to give up?

That moment, that tiny doorway, is all that's needed when you're rebuilding your confidence during your recovery after an accident or injury, whether or not it's related to horses. But it takes paying attention, and it takes a willingness to feel a little bit differently about things, especially when it comes to the miraculous body you're in. I understand that injuries can make it seem as though the body is anything but miraculous. But you can start with your breath, feeling it move in and out of your body, and discover that spark of curiosity about what sustains us all.

FOURTEEN

HEARING THE BODY

For most of my life, I've done my best to listen to horses. During recovery and the rehab of my right leg, I realized that I'd spent the same amount of time *not* listening to my own body. On the few occasions I did, I rarely wanted to act on what it needed. I began to see this accident as a chance to change that pattern.

If I was in pain, I stopped what I was doing and rested. If I felt tired, the same rule applied. And while movement brought relief, there was only so much movement I could handle before I needed to be still again. I've been active much of my life, so listening and acting on this need was not something that felt familiar or comfortable. Underpinning everything, and making it possible, was the knowledge that horses weren't just part of my life. They were also part of who I was.

Through this accident, I discovered that the way to get back to feeling less fearful of horses is to do most of the work away from horses. In the months after the fall, it became clear to me that the paradox of loving horses since I was in diapers while simultaneously feeling an overwhelming fear of them was one I couldn't navigate by myself. My days of rabid independence were over.

My friend Lasell, a therapist, gave me a session with her friend, a trained Somatic Experiencing therapist who practiced nearby. It was a long time before I took Lasell up on her offer, because while I knew that my commitment to horses was stronger than my resistance to facing what happened, it outweighed it only by ounces. The deciding factor was that the pain in my leg had receded, but hadn't gone away. It had set up residence and reminded me every day of what had caused it.

When I gathered my courage and went to my appointment with the frantic chant, "You'll feel better you'll feel better you'll feel better . . ." running through my head, I found a soft-spoken woman who put me at ease. Margaret welcomed me into her office, and after I explained why I was there, we began.

I don't remember most of the particulars of that session, but I do recall that she was careful to be sure the emotions weren't overwhelming me. At one point, with my hands on my still-swollen right thigh, she had me say, "Bree is no longer on my leg."

It was so odd. So unexpected. Of course Bree wasn't on my leg! Yet after I said it, I burst into tears of relief.

It can be intimidating to find yourself in the middle of a maelstrom of emotions—a tornado that's going to carry you far away from everything you know and love. Your brain will give you very sound and logical reasons why locking this up, or ignoring it, would be a Very Good Choice. There's a part of your brain that speaks to you in the smooth and velvet tones of someone who cares about you, who wants to make sure you're not in pain, not scared.

In this instance, however, your brain is a con artist. An illusionist. The house your brain would have you believe is the safest—which, by the way, is itself—is made of straw and will crumple the first time a breeze hits the walls. If we sacrifice or overlook or ignore the healing of stored trauma in the body, the brain's walls of defense are flimsy at best.

Here's the kicker: the tornado you want to hide from is the very storm that will blow away the clouds (in this case, anxiety and fear). This tornado roaring through our nervous system, this need our bodies have to shake and move after an injury, is short-lived. It's not permanent. The intensity causes many of us to fight or brace against what our bodies need to do in order to let it go. Once this happens, all that energy gets stored in our bodies. The con-artist part of our brain allows us to believe that we have "sucked it up" and "moved forward" from the event we felt threatened our existence. We might temporarily feel better until something reminds us that all is not well.

One of the most surprising lessons I've learned is that taking care of the body goes a long way toward taking care of the mind. Up until this accident, I was a great believer in the power of my brain and viewed the body as the means to carry it around. As it turns out, when the body is injured, the brain doesn't function very well either. When we have a brush with our own mortality, it shakes us loose from the belief that we will, in fact, live forever. As the brain sorts through pain signals, it's difficult for it to notice anything else or formulate a plan. It feels like a road trip that gets hijacked by a stalled engine in the middle of a long stretch of desert nowhere.

We wish we hadn't been injured. We wish we hadn't made the choices we did when we were with the horse when it was being a horse and did a big horse thing. Maybe we wish we hadn't started with horses at all. We wish we weren't in so much pain. We wish we didn't have to expose others to that pain, or our weakness, or our perceived ineptitude. We should be stronger, braver, healthier, smarter, more skilled, and on and on.

Where do these thoughts come from, and why do we entertain them? Can you see and feel and hear and even taste how defeatist this line of thinking is? How, when our brains and bodies need a life preserver the most, we are busy yanking it away and telling ourselves to just swim? This is where I often think of my favorite bumper sticker: Don't Believe Everything

You Think. Part of being human is sometimes having these kinds of thoughts, and there's nothing wrong with them. There may even be a good reason for them. But having a good reason for something doesn't always mean that it's good for you.

I know first-hand that feeling better, healing, growth, and joy don't arise from anchoring yourself deep in the riverbed. They arise from stepping into the current and going with it. From choosing which current to float in, and keeping your eyes on the next bend in the river. From finding others who are skilled in swimming that river, and seeing what they have to show or teach you.

Before you think this sounds impossible, before you make your home in a place far away from fast-moving water, I have a simple question for you to consider: Does this help your horse? Does it help your current horse, or any horse you bring into your life, to choose to stay bone-rattling afraid?

Most of us get pretty motivated when it comes to our horses. We do our best for them. A lot of us have the job we have because it allows us to have horses. We're up early in the morning and late at night, walking with them through illness. We go to clinics, buy them things, and spend time learning and feeding, mucking and brushing because connecting with them, these authentic, free and still-wild creatures, somehow unfetters us too. If we are the anchor, they are the sails.

I have found that when I feel unable to do something for myself, if I can think of how it would help my horse, I can do it. Once I do it, I feel so good that I keep looking for other ways to feel better.

After my session with Margaret, the pain in my leg was almost gone. Over the following days, there were times when I didn't even think about it. The mind is a powerful tool and we can wield it for our benefit or to our detriment. If we allow our bodies to also have a voice, the potential for healing is amplified.

It's an odd place to be in, wanting to accept a current physical or emotional challenge and yet also looking for ways to improve. At first glance, you could say that they cannot coexist, that acceptance and self-improvement are at eternal odds with one another.

Until the accident in 2014, I would've said the same thing. Either you accept yourself as is, or you seek to improve yourself.

Here's what I've learned: acceptance of where you are, where you sit and breathe and exist, can go hand-in-hand with finding ways to feel better about where you are going

Any major life-happening changes us. There's no rewind button, and we rarely get second chances. What there is, is our ability to make the best of what we have. In the immortal words of the Rolling Stones, "You can't always get what you want/but if you try sometimes/well, you just might find/you get what you need."

Trying, in my case, meant seeking out people who were knowledgeable in areas I wanted to explore. There were days when staying in bed felt easier, but I tried to balance them out with days of learning and curiosity and getting help.

The passage of time has deepened my understanding of some of the physical limitations I was facing. While I was getting to know those limitations better, I was also figuring out what sorts of things could expand them.

By definition, a limitation is something that limits; restraint.

Now, I'm all for restraint, a valuable quality in so many situations. (Except for dark chocolate.) But who said we have to live by our limitations?

Throughout history, there are examples of great women and men from all over the world who made of their life something greater than themselves. They often faced gargantuan obstacles: race, gender, education, physical ability, circumstance, being ruled by tyrants or pushed on by the majority, or all of these combined. What would our world be like without Amelia Earhart, who not only fought against the gender bias of her time, but got in a plane and flew right through it? Where would we be without Marie Curie and her Nobel Prize–winning research on radioactivity? Where would we be without the examples of courage of Mahatma Gandhi or Nelson Mandela or Rosa Parks? Without the liberating words of Maya Angelou or Helen Keller, or the many writers who created new worlds on the pages of a book? Would we be laughing as much without the gift of Robin Williams' humor? Or be as inspired if we didn't read the story of Malala Yousafzai? Would mathematics be as advanced without Ramanujan, or the team of women mathematicians who did calculations by hand to get the first spaceship to the moon and back? What would our world look like now if Alan Turing hadn't delved into creating a machine that we now call a computer? Would our eyes be as observant if we never saw the images by Georgia O'Keeffe, Vermeer, or Frida Kahlo? Would our ears be duller without the music of Aretha Franklin or Mozart? If we hadn't read Anne Frank or Viktor Frankl's accounts of their lives during Hitler's totalitarian regime, how much harder would it be to get in touch with our own beating hearts and will to live?

There are billions of stories, both told and untold, out in the world, many of them by people facing limitations. No one who rose above them allowed those restrictions to define them, or to stop them from achieving what they wanted to do. Whether our stories are known to others or not, what matters is that we not only know our own tales, but in any given moment are also their author.

During the time I started to take the measure of what I could and couldn't do, I also started thinking about all the different kinds of human experiences there are, and how very fortunate I was. How little I had actually lost. How manageable my limitations were. How, when I thought about the very big picture, the number of things I could do was actually much greater than what I couldn't.

Once I realized that, gratitude was easy. Feeling sorry for myself started to decrease. I started to make friends with my wonky right leg and left-of-center brain. And ate more dark chocolate.

FIFTEEN
FEAR IS TEMPORARY

May 2014

I was sure it was my day to die. Any second, panic was going to eat me alive.

My heart was beating triple time, hammering its way out through the cage of my ribs. What breath I had was trapped in my throat. Unbalanced, I teetered on the balls of my feet and stumbled as I started to walk. I looked at Ally. She was breathing deeply and her eyes were half-closed.

It was a bright and green spring day. We were enjoying a day off before our next set of clinics. Mark was standing in the sandy arena with me and Ally. I'd put a soft bareback pad on her, hoping that it would be more comfortable for my leg than the saddle.

What I was really hoping was that I could get on and she and I could go for a little walk and I wouldn't lose my nerve, or my mind.

As soon as I had this thought, my heart rate sped up, my breath got stuck in my chest, I started sweating, and my hands started trembling. I knew what it was. Part of myself seemed to detach and stand watching as the panic moved through my body.

I now knew enough to start walking, even though I was stumbling in the deep sand. I put my right hand on Ally's neck to steady myself, since walking without my cane was still unfamiliar. She was quiet and calm; her message was so powerful that I could feel it seep into my own body like morning sunlight.

As we walked together, she adjusted her pace to match mine as I concentrated on placing my right foot where it would hold me up. I'm not sure how much time passed, but when we stood still for a moment, I realized that my breathing was more regular, and I felt calmer.

Mark came over and held her for me while I hobbled up the mounting block. I couldn't put weight on my right leg yet, so mounting from the horse's right wasn't going to work. Standing on my left leg, I was grateful that Ally was short and the mounting block was tall. I picked up my right leg by grabbing my chaps and lifting, and promptly hit Ally in the hindquarters. When I looked at her to apologize, I saw that she had barely opened her eyes. It took two more tries before I got my right leg over her and settled into the comfort of the bareback pad. Ally looked as though she'd like to take a nap.

Both Mark and I were grinning. Sometimes there are no words for moments like these, and we shared that response. He asked if I was okay, and for the most part, I was. I was feeling nervous, but not like I did on the ground. He let go of the reins, and after several deep breaths, I asked Ally to walk.

We did several laps together, her moving carefully while I focused on breathing and feeling the contours of the pad and her body moving underneath me. Then we stopped and Mark helped me slide off Ally's right side, supporting me until my left foot came down.

I burst into tears. While most were from happiness, because I had proven to myself that I could once again ride, a few were from the pure relief of surviving the experience.

Looking back, I probably pushed myself to return to riding too soon. My nervous system and brain could've used a few more weeks—or maybe months—to settle down. Perhaps I could've saved myself all that fear and anxiety by going slower.

I won't ever know, and at this point, the only time I think about it is when I'm working with someone who's questioning whether or not they would like to ride. My usual response is to suggest that not riding is also an option. Going slowly is always a solid choice; we learn better when things are slow. Plus, we won't scare ourselves back to the couch and the television.

Here are some of the stages we may go through when we're trying to find our way in difficult spots. We may feel paralyzed (in the mental health field, this is called tonic immobility), we certainly feel anxious (unease or nervousness about an upcoming event, or something that we'd like to do, but aren't sure we're able), and fearful (which the dictionary defines as an unpleasant emotion caused by the belief that someone or something is dangerous, likely to cause pain, or a threat).

Personally, I'd separate nervousness from fear and anxiety, because for me, at least, it's possible to ride with nervousness as a companion. Fear and anxiety, not so much. Nervousness generally is something that happens before anxiety. On my nervous system's volume button, it's a two and anxiety, fear, and immobility are seven, eight, and nine. Nervousness is a trembling in my guts, but I can still think and operate and breathe. Anxiety, fear, and feeling like I can't move steal my breath, my ability to think, and my skill with horses; they try to convince me that life won't ever be fun again. They try to make me see the sense in staying in bed all day. Doing endless rounds of housekeeping or laundry. Answering emails in a way that makes me sound as though I know what I'm talking about.

Whether or not we wish to blaze new trails and leave the trauma road in our rearview is strictly personal. The ways trauma expresses itself and is resolved are entirely individual.

While we have been talking about horse accidents, the broader picture is that trauma doesn't have to be major for us to register and carry it. This is why sometimes, even when a person hasn't had a major accident, or perhaps any accident, with a horse, he or she can fear riding and not know why. As Peter Levine says, "Trauma can, in fact, impact us in ways that don't show up for years."

Sneaky, right? I remember really disliking this part of the regaining-confidence process—that I could neither predict or control when anxiety and fear took over. It was like a surprise party without piñatas, friends, cake, or presents.

However, with help from skilled professionals and other resources, it's possible to move through many of trauma's after-shocks. It's possible to let all sorts of trauma move through you and be on their way. Although they leave traces, they no longer hijack your inner world and strip your party of all that makes it enjoyable.

My suggestions? Find someone who can guide you through these uncomfortable internal spots. As much as you can, keep moving. Breathe through it. Get the kind support of those who understand what you're working on. Get curious about what troubles you. Watch favorite videos. Laugh. Take a walk. Really, anything—anything other than succumbing to the feeling that you have no power to claim what you once loved. Your path through this is your own to make, and the internal landmarks will be specific to your situation. You can make your own way back to your horse, and the joy you find will be yours to keep.

SIXTEEN
THE POWER OF MOVEMENT

When I was working with horses during my twenties, I was told that under no circumstance was I to allow a horse to take his hoof away once I was holding it. This was echoed in the way farriers worked, and I even taught it to others. It never occurred to me to question why we needed to fight with an animal whose survival depends on running and has the strength and power to do so at high speed. So much of what I was taught and observed in those early days had to do with forcing horses to do things that were foreign to their nature.

Years later, when I craved some other way of relating to horses, I saw the wisdom of letting them move if they felt they needed to.

Eventually, I learned that not only is movement beneficial, but directing it, even more so. A horse in flight will feel better if someone is leading him through it. Not only that, a horse will settle and calm more deeply with help. Aren't we fortunate that horses will do this with humans as well as other horses?

The clearest story I have of the benefit of allowing and directing movement features a horse named Azul.

I'd been working with Azul, a Tennessee Walker gelding, and Mikkie, his owner, for about a year. Although he was tense, we'd made good progress helping him slow down and feel a bit better about what was being asked of him. This was the first time that Mikkie and I were aware of a problem on the ground.

"Azul won't stand still for the farrier. He can get Azul's feet trimmed, but shoeing him is a nightmare. When we try to confine him, put him somewhere he can't move, he rears and strikes. This isn't like him at all! You've been working with us long enough—that doesn't seem like him, does it?" I agreed that it was out of character. Even though Azul was on the nervous side, he was kind and had calmed down in the last year.

"We can't get shoes on. Not even close. I had the vet out, and we took X-rays, but everything is fine. We can't find any pain anywhere. I'm not sure what to do next."

As we led Azul over to a nearby round pen, I asked Mikkie more questions. She didn't know if he'd ever had shoes on, but felt they were necessary because she was planning to take him on a three-day ride in a few months, and much of the route covered a rocky area.

I was grateful we had time to sort through this issue, especially since the farrier didn't make a follow-up appointment; Mikkie and her farrier both wanted to wait until they knew Azul was okay with the process. I asked Mikkie to pick up Azul's hoof, which she did without any hesitation or problem. Azul readily lifted his foot and let her hold it without trying to get away. We repeated the process with the other three, and with each foot, he relaxed more.

Mikkie went back to his left front hoof, and this time after she lifted it, I asked her to tap it with the palm of her hand. Azul's head shot up, but he didn't take his hoof away. Again, we repeated this with the rest of his hooves, and though he was tense, he stood. Then I asked Mikkie to lead him around the pen so he could use movement to release tension.

As he spurted out in front of her, she turned quickly to her left and he followed. After a few laps, he relaxed, and we went through the lifting/tapping routine again. He wasn't as tense or worried. After several repetitions, during which Mikkie tapped progressively harder, Azul was standing quietly with his head down.

We took his halter off and left him in the round pen for a few moments so he could move as he needed to. After walking half a lap, he stood quietly by the gate, looking at us while we chatted.

"So," Mikkie asked, "what's going on?"

"What we're doing is establishing a baseline. When Azul feels tension, we're letting him move instead of asking him to stay still. We know he loves moving anyway, so any time we need him to stand still, it's going to be a stretch for him. He can do it, but we need to be sure to mix in movement as a release.

"Most horses find release from pressure by standing still or cessation of movement. For instance, if we're teaching our horse to do a turn on the forehand, we might ask for several repetitions, and when he does them correctly, let him stand and think about it. Azul, however, is one of those horses who releases by moving."

"That makes sense," Mikkie said. "We've let him move a lot in the process of teaching him to stop calmly."

"Exactly! We're now applying that principle to help him learn to be okay with having shoes put on. My hunch is he may never have been shod before, so that's a factor. But by letting him know he's free to move, he can relax enough to stand still."

I asked Mikkie to get a longe line and a small hammer. Then we went back in and caught Azul, attached the line to his halter, and set the hammer down outside the round pen.

Mikkie repeated picking up Azul's feet and hitting them lightly with the palm of her hand. He was relaxed. She worked with all four feet, and when she offered to lead him around, he walked a few relaxed steps and then stopped.

We repeated this process, with Mikkie using her fist to tap firmly on the bottom of his feet. Again, he was calm and didn't need to move.

I asked if I could take a look at this next step and switched places with Mikkie. She handed me the hammer and I asked for one of Azul's front hooves. I tapped lightly three times before he shied sideways away from me and took off running. As she stood in the middle with me, I explained that though we were in a round pen, we had the longe line on so we could maintain a connection to Azul even if he needed to run. We walked with him as he ran, then walked, and eventually stopped. He turned to face us, ears up and looking for all the world like he wanted to ask, "What was that?"

We walked calmly up to him, and I asked for the same hoof we had just worked on. He raised it, and I tapped with my hand first, then put the hoof down. Azul was tense but relaxed quickly. I then tapped once with the hammer, on the outside of his hoof, then put the foot down. Azul moved away, this time walking.

"Good!" I said. "This gives us a baseline. He just told us that he can stand one tap, but no more. From here, this is a really straightforward process. We'll repeat it until he's fine with one tap on each foot and doesn't feel like he has to run away."

Surprisingly, this took a relatively short time. We unclipped the lead rope from Azul's halter and left the round pen so he could move. He paced a few laps, and then stopped at the gate.

That day, we spent more than two hours with Azul, which included the frequent breaks we were giving him. At no point did he rear or strike, choosing only to move away from us before running. By the end of our session, we could tap on all four of his hooves with the hammer, using medium pressure, and he would stand. He hadn't yet reached full relaxation, but neither was his head up and his body tight. Mikkie said she would work a little bit on this every day until I saw them next.

A week later, Mikkie and I were chatting about Azul's progress while he stood with us in the round pen. She showed me how she could pick up each hoof and tap a dozen times all over it with the hammer, then put it down, and he could stand quietly.

"When I worked with him the day after you were here, he had to run again, but I did the same thing we did and walked with him until he could stop, and then we tried again. He got better pretty quickly," she told me.

"That's great! He's doing really well, considering he used to think this was going to be the end of him."

"What's next?" Mikkie asked. "Can we put shoes on him now?"

"Not quite." I'd brought an old horseshoe with me and now I pulled it out of my jacket pocket, along with a handful of hay, which fluttered to the ground. The shoe was rusty but nail-free and balanced.

"Now we'll do everything you've practiced over the last week, but we'll be tapping the shoe as we hold it against his hoof." I asked Mikkie to hold Azul while I demonstrated it.

He quickly gave me his left front hoof, and I held the horseshoe against it; with the other hand, I tapped once very lightly on the shoe.

Although his reaction wasn't as dramatic as it had been in the beginning, he took his foot away as I set it down and loped off. After he'd run a few laps, he stopped.

This time, I put the shoe against my leg and tapped it with the hammer so he could see what the noise was about. Azul scooted off into another lope, during which I kept tapping the shoe. He stopped, looking at me, ears stiffly forward. After I tapped the shoe a few more times, I stopped, too.

I took a few steps closer and tapped the horseshoe with the hammer again. Azul stood still but wasn't able to relax. We repeated this process, with me stopping the tapping when he was quiet and then stepping closer to him until I was standing beside him while tapping the shoe, and he was able to stay still and calm.

Eventually, we could hold the shoe against any of his hooves, tap it lightly, and put the hoof down. By the end of the session, Azul was standing quietly as Mikkie worked on his feet.

When I visited the next week, Mikkie couldn't wait to show me their progress. I followed her into the round pen, where Azul was standing. She caught and haltered him, then handed me lead rope. She took a shoe and the hammer in one hand, asked for Azul's left front hoof, and when he gave it to her, put the shoe against his hoof and tapped above each hole where a nail would go.

Just as I was about to tell her what a good job they both had done, she tapped harder, as though she were driving nails into the hoof. Azul, with his head down, barely noticed.

She let go of his hoof, and turned to me, beaming.

"Wow!" I said, smiling back. "Let's see that on all four hooves!"

The cotton lead rope was loose in my hand as Mikkie moved around Azul, picking up each hoof and tapping over the nail holes. He never moved. When she put the hammer and shoe down and led him away, he walked quietly, without any sign that he needed to run.

The next time the farrier came out, there were no problems. It was an easy time for Azul, for the farrier, and for Mikkie. Because he was allowed to move, he could choose to stand still. Because he didn't need to run and instead understood what was being asked of him, he could relax. Because he could relax, he could be at peace with the process.

SEVENTEEN
PICK A DIRECTION

As our understanding of the brain/body connection evolves, we are learning that there is more interplay between the brain and the body than we'd previously thought.

As a recent example, we're learning that the health of our gut influences our moods. The old adage, "You are what you eat," has been proven true on many levels; it turns out, the way we treat our gut influences our brain. If, say, we live on a diet of sugar (which, to be honest, is my version of heaven) and processed foods with very little or no fresh food, there's a good chance we will create an imbalance that affects how our bodies digest and distribute nutrients. This imbalance in our gut then creates an imbalance in our brain function. Another really interesting thing is that this process goes the other way too; whatever is going on in our mind—say, for example, fear and anxiety after a horse accident—may set up an imbalance in our digestive system.

Recovering from a horse accident is about using this incredible brain we've been given to pursue healing. We replace the statement "I should be able to ride without fear!" with the question "How do I heal as best I can in order to be confident with horses?"—assuming that's the goal we're building toward.

Notice the words "as best I can." This may mean returning to your previous fitness and strength. It may mean surpassing it. Or, it may mean that, given the circumstances, there's only so much healing your body can do. I believe that the body has incredible powers of healing and adaptation. If we can partner our brains with our bodies, a different experience of life is possible.

I've spent far too much time berating my body and wishing it was something different. Wishing I didn't have so many injuries, or that I could be athletic and daring and bold. All that time I spent focusing on my perceived shortcomings could've been used to focus on what I can do. And what I can do these days is more than I ever dreamt of doing when I was in my twenties.

Instead of judging or bemoaning or grieving everything we can't do—all of which are completely normal (if aggravating) mental activities—by switching our mindset, we can use the brain to help the body. To lift it. To offer it any therapy we can find or imagine.

I feel fortunate that I was aware of so many complementary therapies before this accident. Even knowing what I did, I still spent an unfortunate amount of time feeling pitiful, crying a lot, and wondering if my life was gone.

When I told people what happened, I used the word "crushed." That's exactly how I felt in those months after the accident: anything that was me had been crushed. I was an origami bird with an awkwardly bent wing and a crooked neck. Instead of glossy paper plumage, I was wrinkled and bulging in places that should've been smooth and straight.

After spending too much time with these thoughts, the kindness of friends and strangers showed me that there was more to being injured than feeling helpless. I gave in to the peace and calm that wanted to envelop me.

Acceptance felt so much better than self-pity or anger or apathy.

I didn't know if my leg would return to normal (spoiler: it hasn't), I didn't know if I would enjoy or ever feel comfortable with horses again (good news: I do). What I did know was that there was a place inside me that no accident could touch. If I spent my time there and focused on seeing this pain and doubt through, the answers would present themselves.

This is where I started to realize that listening to the body would be helpful. Healing, even. That I could use my brain not to outsmart or ignore my body, but to find ways to support and strengthen it. To find ways to finally unite the part of me I'd always taken pride in—my mind—with the part of me that had always caused me embarrassment because of its shortcomings—my body.

It came down to choosing between staying afraid and avoiding the work that would alleviate fear, or reducing the feelings of fear and find out how far down the road to confidence I could get.

In her recent book, *The Body Never Lies*, Alice Miller says, "Ultimately the body will rebel. Even if it can be temporarily pacified with the help of drugs, cigarettes, or medicine, it usually has the last word because it is quicker to see through self-deception than the mind. We may ignore or deride the messages of the body, but its rebellion demands to be heeded because its language is the authentic expression of our true selves and of the strength of our vitality."

My body had taken a bit of a hit, and I couldn't continue the charade of appearing to be confident while feeling anxious on the inside. And feeling like a fraud. So the choice between living in fear and pursuing confidence now was clear, and I had to make it. One or the other. With horses, or without.

Being with horses is like being in love: you either are or you aren't. For those of us who have been wildly hurt and who also wildly love horses, the prospect of riding after an accident can create a feeling of living in two worlds. In one world, our heart synchronizes to the heartbeat of an animal who is part gentle breeze and part hurricane. In the other, we tell ourselves to be reasonable because we know very well how badly we can be injured. There's no halfway; there's only the decision to be in or out. Being half-hearted with an animal whose reaction time is in the milliseconds is like thinking we can dodge bullets.

Horses require awareness coupled with patience. We will feel better if we have a sense of humor about the differences in our species and have an ability to not only see things clearly but to ask for help if we don't know what is going on.

Sometimes accidents happen even when we are with horses whole-heartedly, and sometimes this takes the heart we have for horses right out of us. However, at some point, we must make the decision to be with horses or to be without them. In or out. It's a decision we will be required to make again and again if we choose to keep spending our life in their hay-munching company.

For the most part, living with paradox is not something we're good at. Although we crave having it all ways—or at the very least, our way—we also have experiences that point toward the peace we will feel if we decide on a course of action. Set our feet on the path. Choose which side of the fence to be on.

As Richard Feynman said, "The paradox is only a conflict between reality and your feeling of what reality 'ought' to be."

Horses are tolerant of many things, but paradox isn't one of them. They're also more honest than we are in their expression of this intolerance. One of the many lessons I am grateful to have learned from horses is this: do one thing or do the other. Not both.

So here we are, back at the fork in the road. Until we figure out how to be in two places at once (the word for this is bilocation), choice and what follows from it will be consistent companions throughout our lives. No matter how big or small, an accident or injury makes our options immediate and clear.

I now feel that accidents can be invitations to leave what once was and explore what can be, which is whatever we wish it to be. We can have horses, or not. We can feel better, or not. We can go back to what we were doing with horses, we can do something different, we can stop riding but explore unmounted activities . . . we can, we can, we can.

Fear and anxiety's only answer is "cannot." If we let this voice shout out the directions, our lives get small and small is safe. While that's true, what's also true is that growth doesn't happen in a space that is too small. Think of a plant: we have to keep repotting it into larger containers it if we wish it to grow. Humans aren't all that different, really, from the rest of nature.

Our bigger containers are of our own making and our own choice. If you enjoy affirmations, go for it. Write and speak them until they permeate your dreams. Meditation? Sit until your bliss shines. Walking? Running? Taking the dogs out and playing? Do it, over and over again. Whatever your way of finding relief is, now is the time to do it wholeheartedly.

And if there's something that interests you but you've never done (for me, it was quilting), give it a whirl. There's this amazing thing called the Internet, which you can use to explore your curiosities any time of the day or night. You can find a bigger container and replant yourself without even getting out of a chair. No bilocation is necessary.

Where does the horse fit into all of this? Wherever you want. Once I had decided that my love of all things horse was still alive and kicking, I started with something easy. Grooming and hanging out near paddocks watching how horses interacted with each other were the two activities that felt manageable to me.

After decades of doing various things with horses, I realized that I had returned to watching and listening to them. But this time, I had decades of learning behind my observations. I started seeing things I had missed before and knew that I was being given a chance to learn, yet again. I didn't particularly like the way the lesson came to me, but sometimes we don't get a say in that. Here was a chance to observe and watch and learn. I took it.

Not all days were like this. There were dark days when I didn't want to talk or think about what had happened. Days when getting dressed and stumbling around was too much. Days when I couldn't sleep or rest and nothing appealed to me. Giving up seemed so much easier, so much more available, than fighting through the rubble of internal and physical misery.

These feelings weren't new—I'd met them when I was still in my teens—but this time, I could add injury to the mix, the need to rely on others all day, every day for help. I've never thought of myself as a proud person, but as the days and months went by, I discovered that I dressed my pride in humility's clothing, and every time I was forced to ask for help, that clothing became a little more threadbare.

It's amazing work this brain of ours does, functioning on so many levels. Hiding so many things. Yet it becomes even more amazing once we're aware of the ways we can enlist it in the care of our bodies. After any kind of accident and/or injury, whether horse-related or not, we can seek out ways to lift the burden of trauma.

Some of these things may sound weird. As in, eating grasshoppers weird. They may not be for everybody and not all of them have much (or any) evidence to support their claims, other than rave reviews from people I know. But every one of them helped me in some way. You may want to explore their possibilities for yourself.

I had acupuncture, massage, energy work, and a whole list of therapies: craniosacral, physical, Somatic Experiencing, hydro (water), and laser. I asked my herbalist/nutritionist Grandmother for help. I consulted with a homeopathy practitioner and did several sessions of eye movement desensitization and reprocessing (EMDR). Reiki, castor oil packs, essential oils, flower essences, swimming, regular check-ins with my doctor, and diet and supplementation were all on my playlist. This exploration was integral to regaining function of my right leg as well as in helping my brain heal.

Some of these places I had visited before. I also chose therapies that were new to me, whether I believed in them or not. I chose to be open to what crossed my line of sight. No healing modality was ruled out.

Through time in a therapy pool, I discovered that the inherent vitality of movement (for example, the transformative power of yoga, qi gong, dancing, and so forth) is a cornerstone in reducing anxiety and fear. In the water, I could spend an hour doing targeted exercises during a time when walking more than 100 feet was exhausting.

If you're unsure of the benefit of movement, I invite you to do an experiment. The next time you feel afraid or anxious, as soon as you can, walk. Go up and down stairs. Jump rope or hula hoop. Lift weights. Wave your arms. Do a dance. Anything! Move in some way, for as long as you need to, and then see how you feel.

Movement is vital to feeling alive and experiencing ourselves in new ways. Ways that reconnect us not only to ourselves but to all of life. Like breath, movement is a broad and sturdy bridge between your brain and your body. The more you move, the clearer you will feel. While social media, gaming, streaming programs, and all sorts of techno entertainment are available for our minds to feast on, we have been making our homes in these bodies for thousands of years. Finding a movement practice that suits you will go miles toward you feeling better. When we move, we breathe, and when we breathe, we start to unlock the cage that fear puts us in. When we move and breathe, we can work toward feeling better, toward feeling less fear, toward reconnecting with ourselves in unforeseen ways. With movement and help from skilled and compassionate people, it's possible to start feeling not only better, but positively lighter.

One of those compassionate people, by the way, is yourself. It's only a choice away, and it's a choice that can be made into a habit. We aren't broken vessels to be repaired, but rather, treasure maps to be explored.

EIGHTEEN
CONTINUING THE RIDE

February 2015

Mark and I, along with our horses Ally and Rocky, were back in Florida, visiting the friends we'd been with when the fall with Bree happened. We were heading out for a trail ride, the same one we'd planned to take the previous year.

A year is a long time. And no time. In a moment or two of delusion, I thought this was a good idea because I also thought I'd worked through the fear and lack of confidence, the sweats and tremors, which by that time I hadn't experienced for months.

As I was saddling Ally, flashbacks of silver-gray fog and the feel of hooves drumming the length of my body flooded through me.

I wanted to cancel the ride and leave. Though leaving was a way of coping that has worked for me for most of my life, I knew that well-worn path didn't lead anywhere but to feeding a lack of confidence in myself.

Instead, I breathed deeply, turned away from Ally, and ran as fast as I could down the long and sandy driveway.

When I came back and was saddling Ally, all my old injuries hurt. I saw Bree instead of seeing Ally. I smelled the sharp tang of sweat running down my body, and I felt my heart racing.

The only thing I knew to do at that point was to move. I

wanted to run again, so I did. I finished saddling and turned and ran back and forth down that long, sandy driveway, not caring who was watching. After several laps, I could walk.

I led Ally to the arena, near the area where we would leave for our ride. I walked her around and around in circles, looking at her frequently and telling myself she wasn't Bree, and this wasn't a year ago. As committed to going on this ride as I felt, I also told myself that it didn't have to happen on this day, or even this year. If I was going to be miserable and fighting panic the whole time, it wasn't worth it to me. Nor was it fair to Ally; I didn't want to take advantage of her good nature.

Only after my heart rate had slowed did I put my foot in the stirrup and swing into the saddle. I kept taking deep breaths and let Mark and our two friends take the lead so Ally could follow. I was riding, in a sense, but Ally's calmness was the reason I could go out at all. She didn't spook, didn't speed up, and didn't seem to care whether she was close to the other horses or not. Mark had his eyes on me too, and between the breathing and feeling supported in all kinds of ways, once we returned, I was smiling. I felt triumphant.

Duey, a friend of mine who is a therapist, describes this process as "borrowing another's nervous system." At first this thought freaked me out; I mean, who wants to come into contact with a nervous system that is going haywire like mine was?

Then I remembered all those years and all those horses who were nervous or worried and how I settled into a calm space, knowing at some point they would follow me there. Those horses, I guess you could say, borrowed my nervous system (perhaps their owners did, too) until they could come back to their own.

From the time Ally and I met, I guess you could say that I was borrowing her nervous system. She was different in the way she responded to the world—I could almost feel her refusing to get worried or upset. Ally's outlook was to observe and see where she could quietly blend in. In the year that I'd known her, she was not only consistently quiet, but modeled an ease in the world that I've seen with very few horses.

The point of this anecdote is to let you know that if you focus just a little bit on what is happening in your internal world (and there are many wonderful, professional, and skilled people who are trained to help you do this, if the thought of it is scary) and name what you're feeling, it will ease the fear. The dark is scary only because we don't know what it contains. Or we think we know what it contains, and we don't care to look at it. The dark is neutral. It's our unexamined fears that make it threatening.

Watch children after they've been scared or have fallen. Most of the time, you'll see that they prefer to move. Even while they're howling and in distress, it's the adult who wants to stop them, hold them, and talk them through their fear. Of course, parents don't want to see their children hurting, and all of these things are important. But once the damage is assessed and the child is comforted, allowing movement is the next step. Once we reach adulthood, we seem to drop the "movement" part; we assess damage, we seek comfort, and then we stay still. This, in effect, traps the energy of the shock inside of us where it doesn't stay hidden, or quiet.

The trigger that re-ignites anxiety, seemingly for no reason, can be anything. It can be a sound, a smell, something we see or even taste. Most people (including me) want to be rid of anxiety as soon as possible, especially when we can't see any apparent reason for it. Honestly, when it comes to horses and recovering from accidents, there are a whole lot of things to be anxious about. I'd be a bit worried if people who made a life with horses didn't have, at the very least, a healthy sense of caution around them.

One thing you might be dealing with is an accumulation of small traumas, which have been released by the big trauma of a horse accident. That was certainly the case with me, when I discovered that a life of sweeping shocks and accidents under my internal rug hadn't made them go away. Out of sight was definitely not out of mind.

No one can reach anything close to peace while in a constant state of fear and anxiety. After all the various therapies I've been through, after all the digging around in places I would rather have left alone, I realized that I had to engage in a body-centered practice and give myself a break from looking inside, looking at the past, looking to see where my interior fault lines were and trying to predict the next earthquake.

I'd been practicing the martial art of aikido for several years by then, and I loved both the feeling of being able to protect myself and the multilayered meaning of the principles. One principle that I found particularly helpful was blending. This is the idea that instead of resisting an attacker's strike, we find a way to meet, direct, and dissipate the energy. This had all sorts of applications to not only my internal work, but to working with horses as well. It has been a touchstone for me all these years, a way to stop resisting myself. Once we can find that place, and develop our skill at navigating it, all sorts of good feelings open up. Walls and dams don't only hold back what we fear. They also hold back the good stuff: connection, awareness, joy.

These days, walking with Mark and our dogs, hiking, yoga, and jumping rope are all staples of my practice. The movement allows me to process what needs to be processed and focus on the immediacy of my working muscles, the beauty of the day, or how I once again feel unburdened, if only for a short while.

NINETEEN

HELMETS

*Spoiler alert:
I won't be trying to convince anyone to wear a helmet.*

Besides the brief times when I was riding in an English saddle, I've never been much of a fan of helmets. When I started riding, they were heavy, hot, and made my head into an embarrassing black-velvet potato.

Once I started teaching full time, I became a great big fan of my great big cowboy hat. It kept me in the shade, was light, protected me from the rain, and even looked cute. My vanity gets in the way of so many things. Including good sense.

I hadn't really changed my mind after the accident. I was wearing my cowboy hat when I went down and planned to keep wearing it as though nothing had happened. Clinging to my stubborn ways even after a traumatic brain injury wasn't the smartest decision on my part. But stubborn and smart sometimes don't always live within shouting distance of each other.

This "no helmet" stance was bolstered by a conversation I had with a doctor right before I was released from the hospital.

"How are you feeling this morning?" The young woman in scrubs and a white coat came in, followed by a gang of medical students as is usual in teaching hospitals. I said I felt better, and asked what I should do to take care of my leg, now that we knew it wasn't broken. "Ice? Heat? Elevation?" I asked.

"Sure," she said. "And take your pain meds. You know, I used to have horses too. I miss them." She smiled at a distant memory while I made noncommittal drugged-stupor sounds.

She then turned to her students and began giving them my history, including what brought me into the hospital. She turned back to me, her ponytail swinging behind her, and asked if I was wearing a helmet at the time of my fall.

"No, I wasn't."

I could tell by the arch of her eyebrows what was coming next.

"It would be a good idea in the future to do that."

The question I asked next still surprises me. I had been awake most of the night, in and out of consciousness. I was sore, tired, medicated, and in desperate need of going home, but afraid of the pain that getting there was going to unleash. So, clearly, my brain was scrambled. Yet, out popped the question: "Did you wear a helmet when you rode?"

She paused a moment and then said, "No, I didn't," before she and her students left the room in a hustle of white coats.

Having this bit of information was all I needed to continue my no-helmet-for-me ways. Even my mother and brother repeatedly suggesting that a helmet would be a really, really good idea wasn't enough to sway me.

Then my friend Morgan, a sister of my heart, called one day to check on me.

After I said no to her question about wearing a helmet and complained that helmets didn't protect me from the sun like my hat did, she said, "You know they make this stuff called sunscreen, right? Besides, how many head injuries have you had in your life?"

I've known Morgan for more than twenty-five years, and one of the things I love about her is that she's direct. She has a highly sensitive BS detector coupled with an even more sensitive and kind heart. She's a force of nature, this sister of mine. Where for much of my life, I've felt like a still pond, she's the wind that encourages the water to move.

Because she seemed genuinely interested, I paused, counted, and said, "Five, including this one."

There was a pause as she thought about this. Then she asked, "Do you think a sixth will be the one?"

"Will be the one what?"

"Will be the one that injures your brain so badly that you aren't you anymore."

I went online and ordered a helmet.

It's a deep ocean blue, the back is flat, it's sturdy, and it has plenty of vents. I also got an orange kayaking visor that I glued to the front so I have more sun protection. When this helmet wears out, I'll get one in purple or pink. Maybe electric punk-rock blue. I was online recently and happy to discover that adult helmets are becoming as fun as the ones they make for kids. It doesn't escape me that this new penchant for color all began with a pink rose cane.

A helmet with a flatter anterior profile was important because of what Mark told me he saw when I fell. I hit the ground pancake-flat on my back; if I'd been wearing a helmet with a rounded back, my head would have landed before my body. This could have broken my neck, paralyzing or killing me. We'll never know for sure, and it was a freak accident, but that didn't mean I was going to wear a helmet with a design that made me nervous.

Mark and I have always taken the position that wearing a helmet is a personal decision. There are many conflicting opinions around this point of view. Some insist that we should (my least-favorite word in the English language) require riders to wear them. Others, like me, know helmets are a good idea, but aren't particularly eager to wear them.

Some of the clinic venues at which we teach do require all riders to wear a helmet; property owners need to protect themselves as well as the riders. Most of the time, our clinics are pretty quiet, but even so, horses are horses and accidents happen. In the UK and Europe, many people wear helmets during groundwork as well.

However, if it's up to us, we avoid making helmets a requirement. So much of our work is focused around not creating braces in the horse or the rider. As instructors, we do our best to guide and direct to the softest solution possible. We like our work to create an open feeling, where riders and their horses learn they can take the pressure off themselves—or in the horse's case, have the pressure come way, way down—and yet still do some really cool things together.

People show up with whatever saddle, bridle, or other gear they usually use. Our job is to make sure that the equipment and the ways the riders use it is as functional and clear for their horse as possible. If we think the horse would be more comfortable in a different saddle or bridle, we will suggest that. Otherwise, we do our best to work with what the riders have chosen for themselves and their horse.

Oddly enough (or perhaps not, given the nature of humans), when children show up for a lesson, their parents have taught them that whenever they are around a horse, they need to wear a helmet. Sometimes those same parents will also take a lesson and not wear a helmet.

Most cyclists I see are wearing helmets, but at least half of the people riding motorcycles aren't.

Now, I could posit all kinds of reasons why this happens, but I'd probably be wrong. Most of the time I don't know people well enough to indulge my curiosity; asking why someone doesn't wear a helmet seems tantamount to inquiring who they voted for in the last election.

For the most part, people who bring their horses to us are in a pretty open frame of mind, and can listen to suggestions to change their tack or equipment. But it would feel very odd to say, "You have to wear a helmet." Kind of like venturing into the same territory as telling a person how to spend their money. Or what religion to follow. Or how to drive. Or to stop smoking.

I'd rather let people make their own choice about helmets. We know what's good for us and what isn't. We know we need to get more sleep, eat in a way that supports a healthy body and mind, refrain from excessive drinking, stop complaining so dang much. Maybe get out and walk once in a while. Life is messy, and it sometimes makes for a messy experience. Part of that messiness is knowing, intellectually, what is beneficial for us but not committing to doing it.

Before this accident, I knew what could happen. I knew people who'd had head injuries. I also knew people who'd broken their hips, arms, wrists, or fingers. After hanging around horses long enough, many of us are quite aware of the potential for harm. And just because horses don't mean to hurt us doesn't make the injury hurt any less. We all know accidents can happen to anyone at any time. Technically, we're adults and are capable of looking out for ourselves. So even while I recognize all of the good reasons to wear helmets, I also recognize that it's a decision we each need to make individually.

For me, it came down to a clear choice: preserving who I am and the organ that's mostly responsible for it, my brain, or run the risk of losing it all. Now, I wear a helmet every time I ride.

TWENTY
SETBACKS AS COMEBACKS

July 2015

The morning began, as many mornings do, with Mark and me cleaning out the large, dusty pen the horses were staying in at the clinic venue. It was now late summer and I'd been walking without my cane for several months.

Two of our horses, Rocky and Rusty, had been together for more than a year and were a quiet pair. Our new horse, Bennie, was still figuring out the clinic horse's job, and we hadn't spent a lot of time with him. He moved with his head and neck straight up in the air, and although he was kind, he also was a worrier.

Mark wheeled the manure cart out of the pen to empty it and I continued to clean. Bennie ambled over to where the other horses were eating and they chased him away. As he ran along the length of the fence toward me, I kept thinking he would break to his right, where there was a big open space. When he was five strides away, I raised the manure fork handle, hoping to catch his eye and shift his direction, which at that time was straight at me.

Well over 1,200 pounds, Bennie is a big horse by anyone's standards. He also can move. Quickly. His head was in the air, the whites of his eyes were showing, and in two strides, he was close enough for me to tap him on the left side of his face with the handle of the manure fork to direct his nose (and his body) to the right.

The next thing I knew, I was spitting out dirt and Bennie was standing in the farthest corner of the pen, sides heaving and dust floating around his hooves. He'd run into me, knocking me to the ground before I knew what happened.

As I lay there, stunned, I took a quick inventory and decided that I was basically okay. I hadn't hit my head, and although my jeans were ripped and my hands scraped up, everything was intact. By that time, Mark had come back and was helping me up. I started crying and shaking, but knew this was a temporary response. I also knew that Bennie, in his panic, had not seen me—probably didn't even feel it when he knocked me down.

Next, I went for a walk, which turned into a run, which then turned into another, slower walk. The shaking came and went, as did the other emotions: anger, fear, frustration. I questioned the wisdom of working around horses. I blamed Mark for buying this horse. I questioned my ability and did I do the right thing and why didn't I get out of the way? I think I may have questioned my whole dang existence on the planet. My biggest fear? That my confidence had been set back yet again.

As I walked, these thoughts came, then went away. It's difficult to beat yourself up when your leg muscles are on fire and you're gasping for air.

When I got back, we went through our day as usual. I stayed away from Bennie to give myself time to process the run-in. The next morning, as we went in to clean the pen, I noticed my heart rate and breathing. They stayed normal the entire time; nothing changed, even when I haltered Bennie and led him to the trailer.

Turns out, all those questions and emotions were passing things—clouds in the sky, not rocks to build my life upon. I didn't need to stop being around horses, I wasn't totally incompetent, and being knocked down wasn't a setback to my healing and confidence.

Several days later, it occurred to me that because I had the opportunity to address the trauma in the moment, it didn't have any lingering effects. I rode my horse with no more fear than I had before. I didn't feel less confident. I wasn't unsure of myself as I taught. Not letting trauma fester was an incredibly straightforward lesson: Let the body do what it needs to. Let the emotions come and go. Move on to the next thing. Straightforward, but I know in many instances, not comfortable or easy.

It's not about thinking our way through the situation. The body needs the chance to complete its process. There's the shock/trauma, there's the result of the trauma, then there's the resolution, which often manifests as shaking or trembling. Once we understand that this is a very old, very necessary part of moving through something scary, we can allow it to happen and not feel so afraid of it. Or ashamed.

We can give ourselves a break and be okay with our humanness, with our fragility, with our stumbling and missteps. I'm not sure how we picked up the notion that being human equals being perfect, but this is one equation we can forget and lead a fuller life without.

TWENTY-ONE

CHANGING FEAR
TO CURIOSITY

I'm the first to admit that there's a lot I don't know. I will also admit that I love being a student. The feeling of not knowing, these days, isn't as intimidating as it used to be.

Here's what I do know: it's 100 percent unhelpful to sit on a horse with your heart racing while you try to reason your way out of the fear that's crippling you. It's the easiest way I know to feel like a failure, to feel weak and cowardly and give credence to those internal voices snickering, "You'll never ride again."

Although the neocortex (the "newest," according to the tri-une-brain theory discussed earlier) will tell us quite confidently that we can ride through our fear—or, even more destructive, that we *should* ride through our fear—our bodies and the oldest part of our brain will not agree. Flight-or-fight will override our neocortex, shunting resources most needed for survival into other areas of our body; other parts of our brain come online and the neocortex essentially goes off. Our amazing brain can be both the screwdriver and the loose screw.

That's why it's so difficult to think clearly when we are in the middle of a crisis. It's also why scaring horses as a regular training practice is not effective. A brain in a fear state, ready to fight or flee, is not a brain that's capable of long-term learning. While we might learn what we're afraid of and how to avoid it, long-term, complex learning becomes much more difficult. It's often why horses we thought were trained will fall apart if the horse is caught between doing what we ask and the instinct to save their own life.

Something interfered with the learning process—stress, pain, worry—so when the horse felt threatened, she returned to instinct. The training only carried her so far. An instinct that has been honed over millions of years will always be stronger than any training we administer that puts the horse in a state of fear or keeps them just this side of panic. Even when we do our best to teach and educate the horse under ideal circumstances—slow, calm, and quiet, knowing that the horse is physically comfortable—instinct will always win. But we have a greater chance of keeping a horse connected to herself if the distance between calm and worry is greater. That requires a training process that takes into consideration who horses are, not what we try to force them to be.

For example, most of us are taught that when a horse is scared of something, we are supposed to make them go up to it and put their nose on it. Then, this conventional wisdom tells us, they won't be scared.

What if, in the horse's world, they are telling us that their life is in danger and our taking them up to the scary thing is, in essence, saying "I don't care if you're scared or you get hurt, you need to touch this thing with your nose."

One of my first horses, Jack, was the unfortunate recipient of this training regime. At the time, I only knew one way to deal with his epic spooking. After he spun and bolted, I would dutifully force him back to the spot and urge him through it, cursing and kicking the whole time, but trembling on the inside because he was so unpredictable and fast. At the time, desensitization was popular, so I started sacking him out with anything I could find. We went on this way for more than a year. Instead of improving, he got progressively worse. He also became harder to catch. I didn't think the two things were related, but I was new to this horse-training stuff and at that time, unwilling to say the words, "I don't know." Thus began my search to find out why, when I was doing everything the experts told me to do, his spookiness increased.

I began by checking if the saddle fit, and, as it turned out, it didn't. I then strayed from my small circle of experts and had an equine massage therapist out. I gave Jack supplements to address any nutritional deficiencies. He got acupuncture, and the same veterinarian who did that also hand-floated his teeth. His feet were big and solid black. I trusted my farrier and knew that Jack was sound.

The spooking got less frequent, but no less explosive. On the trail, I could count on at least one spin-and-bolt. It happened even in the arena; looking back, I can see that Jack would've done great in a reining pattern if there had been an improv class.

At a clinic, I learned how Jack might be perceiving being forced to go back to the spot where he thought he'd lose his life. In his way, he was telling me he was scared, and in my way, I was telling him I didn't care. He was saying that a sight or sound or smell might kill him. My cursing and kicking and forcing him to face it said it didn't matter, and he'd better do what I say. (For the record, I wasn't actually thinking about any of that. I was frustrated and scared.)

I know now that humans can be clueless when it comes to communicating with horses, even when we don't mean to be. Back then, I started to wonder if my being so emotional could be a part of his spooking so violently. It dawned on me that Jack could be more unsure of our relationship, and thus my ability to navigate us through a scary situation, than of any specific trigger. After all, if I couldn't hear him when he was practically advertising in neon that he was scared for his life, why would it be a good idea for me to be on his back, directing him where to go?

In addition to taking care of his body, I began to ignore his spinning, spooking, running backward, and attempts at bolting. I rode him in the direction we had been going, but if he wanted to detour around something, I let him. I redirected his spinning so he couldn't run off. Instead, we did a lot of small circles and figure eights. I never asked him to stand still, but otherwise I ignored everything. My job was to remain calm and understanding, and most of the time I could do that. I also stopped all the desensitizing work, no doubt much to his relief.

Jack had a way of throwing me a look that eloquently communicated exactly what he was feeling. After he was done spinning and we had worn a figure-eight pattern in the dirt, he would slow to a walk, take a deep breath, and look back over his shoulder at me. It was as though he were saying, "That's it?"

We went through a couple of months of the old pattern, but I refused to give in to my habits of fear, anger, and frustration and instead focused on the signals and clues Jack was giving me and how I might respond in a way that would help him feel better. I rode through the spin, redirected the energy of the bolt, and we went on our ride. Then he started to get quieter. It began to feel as though his hooves were actually touching the ground, a new sensation for both of us; to me, he'd always felt like a hovercraft.

When I look back on it, what we were really working on, the most crucial piece of the whole puzzle, was trusting each other. It took years for that to happen, and Jack was a saint in horse's clothing to put up with my many mistakes and my messy emotions. Years later, this was a horse I could ride bareback on Arizona trails, and later, trails in my new home state of Colorado. We went through some rough times together, and those experiences forged our belief and trust in one another.

For both Jack and me, switching fear to curiosity took a very long time, which probably had more to do with my then-mindset than anything going on with him. Once he was feeling physically better and I started to understand things from his perspective, we were both less fearful. When that happened, I could feel his reactivity going away, and things that once scared him weren't an issue. He would walk by them or on them or around or under or through them with barely a blink. His version of curiosity started to look a whole lot like bravery.

Looking back gives us perfect vision. I now know that the relationship Jack and I shared was far more valuable to me than anything we did together. When he was older, we still went on trail rides and hikes, Jack wearing only a halter and eager to get out. But what I treasured most was being with him, just spending time with this horse who had gone from suspicious, in pain, and confused to being one of my greatest teachers.

Because of his confidence, I was able to celebrate my own moments, times when something that used to scare me showed up and I wasn't scared. Or my growing ability to think clearly in a previously nerve-racking situation. Maybe my curiosity started to look like bravery, too.

TWENTY-TWO

LITTLE POSITIVES

As I write, a cup of tea on my left and my old cat curled up on my right, I realize that my accident and injury were life-changing in ways that I'm still grateful for. My courage feels expanded; my tolerance of myself and others has grown; and most days, I feel calmer than I have since my twenties.

On days I'm feeling nervous about being with my horse, I follow the patterns I've developed. They include not only what I've written about in these pages, but also, anything new that's caught my curiosity. The results are consistent: I feel better.

I've always said that if I died while being with horses, I would die happy. The fall with Bree was a little too close to that sentiment for comfort, but it did remind me of my own mortality. In addition, it also gave me a better sense of my shortcomings, my regrets, and the places I've resisted growth. These are part and parcel of my acceptance of my strengths, resiliency, the ability to articulate things I feel passionate about, and a new-found knack for finishing what I start.

When thinking about all the things that have contributed to my current state of mind, I realized that it's not just about my triumphs; it's also about my mistakes. How the things I think expose my weakness and frailty, the things that have me convinced I can never do anything again, are also the blueprints I can use to step forward into the unique gifts I have to offer. Every mistake is actually a part of learning and improving.

I don't watch a lot of television, but on one of my favorite shows, there's a guy who shares his wisdom in a way that's real and feels not only manageable, but inspiring. In one episode, he said that his grandmother once told him that failure isn't the opposite of success. It's part of it.

It isn't too different with horses. With a little persistence and patience with ourselves, we can go as far as we want with them. At the time of this writing, I'm five years away from the accident and am now taking jumping lessons on Rocky. I wasn't sure I was going to make it this far, but I have. It's been a step-by-step, sometimes a minute-by-minute, process and while in it, I've done my best to listen to my body and use my mind for my benefit instead of letting fear tear me down to its level.

Where does it begin? With us. With being aware of the messages our body is sending. With taking deep breaths. With taking more deep breaths. With being able to relax a little bit. I'm not sure you could call it meditation, but every morning before I get out of bed, I do a quick scan, feeling what may be happening inside of me. At some point during my day, I'll do another scan. I also do this before going out to catch my horse. It helps me know where I can do my best work on that day. Some days, it's from the ground, and others, it's on the back of a horse. Some days, we stay in a walk and practice lateral work, other days, we canter. There's a particular freedom in not having anything to prove, a freedom that comes from making your internal environment just as important as your external.

My friend Gray, one of our student instructors, was at a clinic in Texas. At that clinic, a white pop-up tent sheltered a table with paperwork, snacks, and extra water. On the first morning of the clinic we walked up to it and greeted our hosts, who asked how we liked the check-in tent. Gray said, "I think we need a check-in tent at every clinic. You know, a place where you can go and say 'I'm feeling a little confused, a little lost, and maybe a little nervous about riding in front of people. Thanks for letting me check in!'" All of us laughed.

Sometimes that's all we need—a check-in tent within ourselves, a place where we can admit what is going on, look at it, and then decide how we'd like our day to run. This doesn't make us weak or odd . . . even if it did, who cares? Make your tent purple or red or blue, sit yourself down just for a moment, and figure out what's ticking inside of you.

Despite what you may have believed, heard, been told, or experienced, you are not a "bad" horse person. You aren't without talent or skill. These things may be clouded by fear, anxiety, nervousness, and doubt, but their opposites can also take root and grow: confidence, relaxation, and surety of purpose. We may only feel just a little of the latter, but we can work with little. We can step into those places where we feel a little bit of joy, a little bit of confidence, and work right there. Little positive places are where the potential is. That is how you will design your own way back to horses.

There was a point after my accident that leading a horse without being nervous about it was quite a big step for me. Grooming, always one of my favorite ways to spend time with my horse, became fun again. When I longed a horse, I went from being afraid of losing my footing to feeling curious about all the subtle ways my horse and I could connect.

I have found that fear, doubt, and all those things that keep us from seizing what we love with both hands are easy to make habits of. I have had days and weeks of having so little energy I didn't want to engage with people or horses or myself. Full days I spent crying, it seemed, from the physical and emotional pain. I wanted to give up everything and find a neutral job where I could coast, where I didn't have to think much, or be much, to anyone.

There are all kinds of terms for this, depression being the

most common. While I've fought this most of my life, I have also come to understand that as helpless and weak as I have felt at times, there has always been something to inspire me to feel differently. Many times, it was being around horses. There were days after my accident when my only tether to life was my work. In the midst of needing help myself, I was also able to help horses and people. In return, I found that I am stronger than I thought. People have endless capacity for kindness and compassion and horses' very presence—their smell, their sounds, and the sight of them—is a fertile oasis that nourishes us as long as we need it.

It's easy to stay at home. It's easy to watch others and long for what we think they have. It's easy to whittle our lives down to a very narrow box instead of focusing on the question: what is it that I *can* do?

If we think of this time in our lives as an opportunity to explore, rather than listing all the ways we have failed in the past and how we are failing now, and how we will always fail everyone and everything and all of life, we could come up with some ways that would help us move out of that pit of failure.

After a lot of digging, I found that indulging my sense of failure was a cop-out. It stopped my learning process, and we are beings who are hardwired to learn. Indulging in thoughts of failure gives us an easy way out. After an accident, man, is it ever easy to chalk it up to failure and move along to something else. We are bruised and battered and broken inside, and sometimes outside, and slipping into failure's warm water is soothing. We get a free pass to leave behind what just happened, because we failed. Because if this happened, then it must mean we aren't any good at it, we will never be good at it, and it's just time to go do something else.

In the light of an accident with a horse, it's normal to re-evaluate and question the wisdom of being so intimately involved with these fast and powerful creatures. If our internal rug looks like a small mountain range, we will often make decisions about horses and about our lives as though standing at the bottom of

Mount Everest, looking up and thinking we will never, ever be able to climb it.

If we can get curious about what is troubling us and take active steps to at least understand it, we can begin making clearer decisions. Decisions that give our heart more voice and our fear much less. After all, we didn't get into this whole horse life so we could be afraid all the time. We didn't sign up for early mornings and late nights and sometimes heavy responsibilities so we could tell our friends what a great day we had being afraid of our horse.

Ironically, now that I feel more confident, I no longer feel the need to ride. I don't feel I have anything to prove, just a lot to share. So that "failure" of coming off horses since I was ten years old is part of who I am today.

Our reasons to be around horses are as varied and unique as we are. Our reasons are also as human as we are. Whatever the reason, choosing a life with horses includes choosing to show up for the rough parts. There is plenty of joy to be had, and once we take a little look at those rough parts, more joy shows up. A little positive, a little joy, a little personal triumph is all we need to take the next small step. Who knows where this will lead us! Maybe to a dead end, perhaps to an open field, most certainly to another challenge, but wherever we find ourselves, we will be there, in our totality, inhabiting this messy and overeager life that is our own.

When it comes down to it, there is only the exploration of how you want to live, as Mary Oliver puts it, "your one wild and precious life."

If there is a cosmic scale when we exit this world, I hope mine weighs out pretty evenly; that the things I fell short on and the mistakes I made are a little lighter than my good decisions. That the acts that have caused harm or hurt in the past are balanced by the kinder choices I tried to make each day in the present. Whether I exit this life because of a horse doesn't much matter anymore. What matters is that between now and the day my time here ends, I can live with more joy than fear, more ease than anxiety, and more acceptance and less judgment.

Perhaps that's all there is to it, this crazy stuff with horses. Figuring out what's important to us and then doing it. Listening to our own voices and listening to our horses, deciding what our priorities are and then living that way. My hope is that if I ever have to return to diapers, there will still be a horse I can spend time with.

And finally, like Christopher Robin to Winnie the Pooh, I say to you, "Promise me you'll always remember: You're braver than you believe, and stronger than you seem, and smarter than you think."

AFTERWORD

FULL CIRCLE

In the pink light of an Arizona morning, Rocky's red coat gleamed. He was sure that standing still wasn't a great idea. He didn't think carrying his head a bit lower was a great idea either. A horse was moving around him and he felt he needed to move, too. Mark, who was riding him that morning, asked Rocky to bring his head down, so down it came, then right back up so he could scan beyond the arena. Mark asked him to stop, and he did. Then, with a swish of his chestnut tail and a little dancing of his white-socked legs, he started moving again.

It was January 2007 and this was Rocky's first clinic. He had a lot of firsts that month. It was his first time as a clinic horse, and the first time traveling so far. It was the first time he'd been away from the ranch where he was born and raised. It was the first time he was asked to stand still in an arena, when most of what he'd known was open range and cattle and long trots.

For three of the four days of the clinic, Rocky moved. He kept a sharp eye on things. For three days, Mark asked Rocky to stop softly and bring his head down a little lower. They did circles and figure eights, Mark guiding Rocky's movement until there was a moment of stillness. Although those moments were punctuated by his dancing legs, the moments grew longer and his ability to relax during stillness stretched out from seconds to minutes.

During lunch on the fourth day of the clinic, I watched as

137

Rocky, saddled and tied to a hitch rail, very carefully lay down and took a nap. Learning how to be calm was hard work.

In June of that year, Rocky and I began working together. I did my best to continue the work Mark had started, practicing softness during the walk, softness at the halt, and softness at different speeds of the trot.

Since I'm built close to the ground, Rocky and I worked on him picking me up from the fence, a skill that to this day he's eager to offer. Back then, we took our time as he went from holding his head up and standing on his toes to sidling up to the fence, putting his head down, and waiting for me to swing a leg over.

We worked together in clinics across the country, practicing stopping softly, turning without rushing, and—the skill that any good clinic horse needs—standing calm and still. Over time, I could count on Rocky to be solid whether we were teaching one rider and one horse at a clinic or riding in a coliseum at a horse expo.

Over dozens of trips and many years of traveling with Rocky to New Hampshire, California, Florida, Minnesota, Washington, Oregon, Kansas, Wisconsin, Utah, and every state in between, we found him to be a confident and willing work partner. He became softer than I had ever felt in a horse; many times, he was so attuned that I learned to notice where I was unclear in my communication with him. Rocky and I were now learning from each other, but I'm quite sure I got the better end of the deal.

In the summer of 2016, more than two years after my almost life-ending accident, I decided I'd like to try cantering. We were home, it was a sunny summer day, and I felt more anticipation than fear when I thought of cantering. Cantering has always been one of my favorite things to do with horses—the power that comes from them and through my body links me to the sky, the three-beat rhythm of the horse's hooves, the swell of breath, and the lift of that moment when both of us are riding the air feels like we leave the earth behind.

I'd been feeling more confident about riding for months. Over breakfast, I let Mark know I was ready to ride another horse besides Ally. Up until that point, Ally and I had walked and trotted. I knew she was okay with a rider at the canter. I knew I would probably also be okay. But I also knew that my mind was again at odds with itself. One part was telling me things would be fine, the other part was flashing code red at the thought of going fast while sitting on the back of a horse.

The first step I took to switch that alarm off was to choose Rocky rather than Ally. When I thought about our history together, I could feel myself calming down. He and I had cantered together dozens of times in arenas and on sandy trails, and I had no question about whether we could do it again.

By the time Rocky was saddled, the day was warmer. I practiced breathing, took a walk before I got on him, and looked down at him to reassure myself that here was the same horse I had spent years riding. Rocky had never offered anything other than an honest effort to understand and work with his rider.

Every time I asked Rocky for a faster trot so I could see if going faster really was an okay thing, I could feel The Freeze come on: my body stiffened, my breath stopped, and my vision narrowed down until I felt I was looking through binoculars. We practiced different speeds in the trot until those things reversed and I could feel the swing of my rib cage match Rocky's ground-covering gaits.

As Mark and I chatted that evening, I said that I'd like to try again the next day, and asked if he would keep an eye on me when I cantered with Rocky, to give me a verbal "all's well." I didn't have any doubts about Rocky. Still, I doubted my own internal system, which had seemed to have shorted out earlier that day when I thought of going faster. I knew that if I heard "You're okay," from someone I trusted, I could quiet that worry.

The next day began as the previous one had, only this time I didn't need to take a walk before riding Rocky. We rode into the arena and started practicing the walk and trot. After several minutes, as we trotted by Mark, I said, "I'm ready. Can you let me know if it's okay to . . ." and before the word "canter" came out of my mouth, Rocky had picked up a soft, slow, steady three-beat gait. It was like he was carrying eggs and didn't want to break them. The canter was so slow and careful that it would have been almost impossible to be scared. I burst out laughing.

We cantered again and again, Rocky moving with a little more energy and speed each time. It felt as though he was continually asking if I was okay. Each time my answer was "yes!" My world became his flying red mane, his hoofbeats on the earth, and the knowledge that he had once again taught me how to fly.

Rocky and I had come full circle. After years of being shown how to live a life on the road, after years of our fostering in him a calm and quiet way of going, Rocky returned that gift to me not only in presence, but also in heart. In a way, he was giving me the feeling we had been sharing with him for years: all is well, and you're okay.

THANKS

After half a century of riding this planet around the sun, I have much to be grateful for. For horses, naturally, but also for the people in my life who have buoyed me up when I felt ready to sink.

I am grateful for my husband Mark, who has supported and loved me through my best and my worst. For my mom and brother, who were and are my first examples of what love looks like and what love does. Another great big debt of gratitude is owed to my mom for not only giving me life but helping give life to this book with her well-honed editing skills. It wouldn't be what it is without her expert guidance.

For my mentor Charlotte McGuire, who chanted the mantra, "Stand in your power and speak your truth," until I actually could. For my sisters Robbie and Cody at the Buffalo Woman Ranch who offer a sacred sanctuary for healing and their cherished friendship, lifelong gratitude for the both of you and all the ways you have supported me in my journey.

To Hunter Purdy, who is a constant reminder of the power of love and soul sisterhood.

Deep gratitude to Anna Blake, the type of friend who can deliver a benevolent kick in the butt and have it feel like a truth that can't be ignored. Your kind insistence and guidance helped put the finishing touches on these pages.

For Tessa and Kristin and Duey, friends who gave their time and heart and skill to this project to help make it better.

For my girlfriends, the sisters of my heart, without whom I

would be lost. Thank you. Whether I name you or not, you're here in these pages, and I am honored that you're also in my life with such presence and kindness. Where would we be without our tribe? I'm grateful I don't have to find out.

To the therapists of all sorts who walked with me through some dark and dangerous times and helped me find clarity; I am where I am because of your excellent work.

Finally, I am grateful for the students who have come to me with their horse and bared their souls. Or included me in a belly laugh. Or hugged me because words didn't come close to how they felt. This book is for you, too.

RESOURCES

Daniel Amen, MD. *Change Your Brain, Change Your Life*. New York: Random House, 1998, 2015.

Christine Barakat. "Sleep Deprivation in Horses." *Equus*. https://equusmagazine.com/horse-care/horse_sleep_deprived_092308-10689. Posted 9/23/2008, updated 7/25/2019.

Pema Chödrön. *Fail. Fail Again. Fail Better*. Boulder, Colorado: Sounds True, 2015.

Donna Farhi. *The Breathing Book: Good Health and Vitality Through Essential Breath Work*. New York: Owl Books, 1996.

Elizabeth Gilbert. *Big Magic: Creative Living Beyond Fear*. New York: Riverhead Books, 2015.

Peter Levine, Ph.D. *Healing Trauma: A Pioneering Program for Restoring the Wisdom of Your Body*. Boulder, Colorado: Sounds True, 2005.

———. *In an Unspoken Voice: How the Body Releases Trauma and Restores Goodness*. Berkeley, California: North Atlantic Books, 2010.

———. *Waking the Tiger: Healing Trauma*. Berkeley, California: North Atlantic Books, 1997.

Bessel van der Kolk, MD. *The Body Keeps the Score: Brain, Mind, and Body in the Healing of Trauma*. New York: Penguin Books, 2014

Made in the USA
Monee, IL
04 December 2019